THE REFERENCE SHELF

Vol. 32   No. 4

REPRESENTATIVE AMERICAN SPEECHES: 1959-1960

Edited by
LESTER THONSSEN
Professor of Speech
The City College of New York

THE H. W. WILSON COMPANY
NEW YORK   1960

PREFACE

If, as Emerson said, "every man is eloquent once in his life," a true history of public address should eventually include some account of the utterances of all mankind. In effect, of course, it does. Oratory, like politics, usually delegates its decisive functions to the more gifted—to those whose moments of eloquent expression are perhaps longer and more frequent than are ordinarily accorded to the average man. The leaders, the small company of men and women in the public view, come to voice the hopes and fears and wants of the many. Accordingly, their words are most likely to appear in the anthologies.

The compiler of selected addresses soon discovers, however, that the vocal output of even this small group of leaders in the several departments of public life assumes staggering proportions. This is not a statement of regret. Rather, it is reason for rejoicing. But it prompts the compiler to speak with candor about his undertaking. It is manifestly impossible for anyone, even with the help of well-disposed friends, to hear, read, or get hold of all the relatively important speeches delivered during a twelve-month period. The best he can do is to choose, with what he hopes is discernment and prudence, a small number of *selected* talks from among those he has examined. The final compilation will not necessarily contain the "best" speeches; such a claim presupposes that the compiler has examined virtually all the talks given during the year, which he clearly has not. Moreover, the speeches are not necessarily "representative." It would require more speeches than appear in this volume to reveal faithfully the many aspects of the many issues that have confronted the country in the last year.

In making the selections, the compiler has been guided chiefly by two standards:

1. Is this a speech one likes to listen to, or read? This is indeed elementary, basic. But it is the point of beginning.

2. At the more sophisticated—the very complex—level, the choice turns on two inquiries: (a) Does the speech express an idea of importance or urgency, one that makes a difference in the lives of Americans? (b) Does it express the idea and mood with a measure of rhetorical distinctiveness?

This is the twenty-third annual volume in the series, and the first under new editorship. Professor A. Craig Baird started the compilation in 1937. After twenty-two years of wise and successful management of the project, he resigned last spring to devote more time to other writing and teaching duties.

LESTER THONSSEN

July 1960

CONTENTS

GLOBAL JOURNEYS OF GOOD WILL

THE EUROPEAN TRIP [1]

DWIGHT D. EISENHOWER [2]

"To give you first my most memorable impression—It is that the people of Europe have a deep liking for the people of America." These words sounded the dominant note of President Eisenhower's report to the nation on his European tour extending from August 26 to September 7, 1959.

During the two-week visit, the President conferred with Chancellor Adenauer, Prime Minister Macmillan, and President de Gaulle. He also had talks with the Prime Minister of Italy and the President and Secretary General of the NATO Council.

On August 25, the day prior to his departure, the President had remarked at a White House news conference that his proposed trip had several purposes, chief among them "To pledge, once again . . . America's devotion to peace with honor and justice; to support Western unity in opposing, by force if necessary, any aggression; and to preserve the defensive strength required for our common security." In this speech he commented on the hopes, stirred by his visit, of providing additional groundwork for "responsible negotiation" of the issues separating the East and the West.

The fifteen-minute address was delivered to the nation from Washington over radio and television on September 10.

Good evening, my friends:

In these next few minutes, I should like to talk to you mainly about my recent European trip.

To give you first my most memorable impression—It is that the people of Europe have a deep liking for the people of America. This they made manifest in a number of ways. In the villages, towns, and in the big cities, I could feel this message rushing across the Atlantic to you. Along the lanes and country roads the message was always the same. Even during a long

---

[1] Text "as actually delivered" furnished by Mrs. Anne Wheaton, associate press secretary to the President, with permission for this reprint.

[2] For biographical note, see Appendix; for references to earlier speeches, see Cumulative Author Index.

automobile trip to make a courtesy visit to the Queen and to her family, there was scarcely a hundred-yard stretch of road that did not have its little knot of people to send back this same greeting and this same sentiment to America.

During the past two weeks I have conferred, as you know, with Chancellor Adenauer of Germany, Prime Minister Macmillan of Britain, and President de Gaulle of France, all old friends of mine. I talked with Prime Minister Segni of Italy; also with Mr. Luns of Holland and Mr. Spaak of Belgium who are, respectively, the President and Secretary General of the NATO Council.

These men are statesmen. Like us, they are dedicated to preserving the security of free nations and to upholding the values we place above all others—freedom, equality of opportunity, human dignity, and peace with justice.

With them we reaffirmed our unity on fundamental issues and in support of the North Atlantic Treaty Organization.

There will be no retreat from the fundamental objectives to which we are collectively pledged. We agreed that the defensive strength required for our common security must continue to be maintained.

For the face-to-face reaffirmation of this faith and purpose, I am grateful and deeply gratified. I had the same feeling during my entire journey, in talking to President Heuss of Germany, and great numbers of other men and women in and out of government.

To our friends in Bonn, London, and Paris, I expressed America's concern over the aggressive actions of the Communists in Asia. Each believed that the United Nations should take official notice of the Laos situation and that we should support that body in seeking a satisfactory solution. Mr. Macmillan was especially emphatic on this point. I am happy that the United Nations has already designated a fact-finding commission of neutral observers. I hope that this prompt United Nation action will serve to halt the aggression that has threatened the freedom of Laos.

Quite naturally much of our discussion centered about our defensive alliance, NATO. All expressed approval of its growing capability to secure cooperation among member nations in political, economic and scientific areas, as a supplement to its work in the security field. The Common Market and similar developments tending to knit more closely together the nations of Europe, also engaged our attention.

One subject involved in our discussions was that of the growing problems faced by the underdeveloped or newly-formed nations of the world. More than one billion needy people require real advances in education, health facilities and living standards. There is an understandable ferment among them—an intense dissatisfaction with their present lot and an increasing determination to improve that lot. They must have greater technical assistance in all fields, large amounts of investment capital, and wider opportunities for trade.

Since all of us outside the Iron Curtain want such progress to be achieved in freedom, the highly industrialized free nations must find effective means to provide the needed help. Each of us has undertaken to study this vast problem which could eventually become a menace to our own freedom. No one nation alone should or can bear the burdens involved, we see again in this matter the need for cooperation and unity among ourselves so that, through equitable sharing, success can gradually but surely be achieved.

In connection with this world-wide issue, I had in Paris a unique and most interesting opportunity to learn many things about political developments in all parts of French Africa. To that city had been invited the prime ministers of the countries making up the French Community. Eleven came.

They were so anxious to express in some unique form their admiration, liking and respect for the people of America that they sent through one of their number, Prime Minister Youlou, a baby elephant. The baby elephant, I understand, is on its way here now, and I shall have to find for it a home in one of our zoos.

The people of these regions who are, in local affairs, largely self-governing, are being helped by France in their economic, cultural and political progress. They have been assured by

France of the right to make their own final decisions as to their own political destiny.

The morale of all these men is high. They repudiate the false teachings of communism. They have a vision of progress and future greatness in freedom. They emphatically expressed to me their gratitude to France and General de Gaulle for the opportunities opening up before them.

It was in this kind of atmosphere that I talked with our Western allies about the impending visit of Chairman Khrushchev to the United States.

I outlined to them the reasons for my invitation to him, which are simply:

First, to give him the opportunity to see what America and Americans are like; to let him see and feel a great and thriving nation living in real freedom.

Second, to give him, face to face, the basic convictions of our people on the major issues of the day, including West Berlin, and to hear from him directly his own views on those issues.

I assured our allies in private conversations, as I have on other occasions publicly, that my invitation to Mr. Khrushchev does not contemplate merely a ceremonial visit—just as it does not suggest any purpose of reaching definitive negotiations. But it does imply the hope that serious exploratory efforts may reveal new opportunities for practical progress toward removal of some of the causes of world tensions.

Conversations with Chairman Khrushchev will not include any negotiation concerning subjects that directly relate to the interests of our allies or to any other part of the free world.

In this connection, I know that neither America nor her allies will mistake good manners and candor for weakness; no principle or fundamental interest will be placed upon any auction block.

This is well understood here and abroad.

Allied leaders expressed their understanding of the reasons that prompted the invitation to Mr. Khrushchev to visit America. While their hopes for progress revealed varying degrees of optimism, each was convinced that the effort was clearly one that had to be made.

Incidentally, I have every confidence that our people will greet Mr. Khrushchev and his wife and family with traditional American courtesy and dignity. We cannot fail to accord him the same consideration which the Soviet public gave to Vice President and Mrs. Nixon.

Having just returned from France, it might be appropriate to recall a comment made about our nation over a century ago by that remarkable observer, Tocqueville. He said, "The great sustaining force of America is not simply to be found in its laws or institutions—but in the manners of her people, her habits of heart."

Each of the leaders with whom I talked is fully aware of America's conviction that any agreement to hold a Summit meeting must be based upon the certainty that our status and rights in Berlin will be respected. In addition, we believe there must be some clear Soviet indication, no matter how given, that serious negotiation will bring about real promise of reducing the causes of world tensions.

Should a Summit meeting on such a basis ensue:

We and our allies stand ready always to negotiate realistically with the Soviets on any mutually enforceable plan for a reduction in armaments.

We are prepared to make a real beginning toward solving the problems of a divided Germany.

We are hopeful of arranging for wider contacts in ideas, publications, persons and information.

We are, in short, ready to negotiate on any subject within the limits dictated by the dedication of our government and our people, to the cause of a just peace, and our loyalty to the United Nations and to its basic concept. That concept is that international disputes should be settled by peaceful means, in conformity with the principles of justice and international law.

I repeat, we shall not retreat from these ideals or principles or weaken in our resolution to remain strong in their defense. This means that we must be as concerned about the freedom of two million West Berliners as we are about the freedom of any part of our coalition.

We must be concerned about threats to freedom, no matter where they may occur.

Though specific problems may at times present such difficulties as to prevent immediate, practicable solution, yet we must all understand that wherever freedom is denied or lost—whether in Asia, Africa, the Americas, or in Eastern Europe—by that much is our own nation's freedom endangered. Firmness in support of fundamentals, with flexibility in tactics and method, is the key to any hope of progress in negotiation.

The choice before world leaders is momentous.

In the past, conferences have all too often been characterized by suspicion, threat, and stubborn prejudice, and results have been barren and bleak.

But, could we create an improved atmosphere of mutual understanding and serious purpose, it would be possible to attack, with renewed hope, the problems that divide us. If the Chairman of the Council of Ministers of the USSR has constructive ideas and suggestions that could provide the basis for responsible negotiation on the issues that divide us, we would welcome the opportunity to study them with our allies.

It is my profound hope that some real progress will be forthcoming, even though no one would be so bold as to predict such an outcome.

Fellow Americans, we venerate more widely than any other document, except only the Bible, the American Declaration of Independence.

That Declaration was more than a call to national action.

It is a voice of conscience establishing clear, enduring values applicable to the lives of all men.

It stands enshrined today as a charter of human liberty and dignity. Until these things belong to every living person their pursuit is an unfinished business to occupy our children and generations to follow them.

In this spirit we stand firmly in defense of freedom.

In this spirit we cooperate with our friends, and negotiate with those who oppose us.

If the forthcoming visit of Mr. Khrushchev to this nation should bring to him some real appreciation of this spirit and this conscience, then indeed the venture would be a thousandfold worth while.

I know that all America prays to the Almighty that this might come to pass.

Thank you, and good night.

RADIO-TELEVISION ADDRESS FROM MOSCOW [3]

RICHARD M. NIXON [4]

In late June 1959, First Deputy Premier of the Soviet Union Frol R. Kozlov (now in the Secretariat of the Soviet Communist party Central Committee) came to New York to open the Soviet Exhibition of Science, Technology and Culture. During his two-week stay, Kozlov conferred with President Eisenhower and Secretary of State Christian A. Herter, and visited cities, farms, and industrial plants across the country. On July 23, Vice President Nixon left for Moscow where on the following day he opened the American Exhibition, thus completing a reciprocal visit.

In his address at the opening of the exhibition, Nixon remarked that "the Soviet Exhibition in New York and the American Exhibition which we open tonight are dramatic examples of what a great future lies in store for all of us if we can devote the tremendous energies of our peoples and the resources of our countries to the ways of peace rather than the ways of war." During the next two weeks, the Vice President engaged in frank conversations with Premier Khrushchev regarding this prospect. Moreover, he traveled extensively in the Soviet Union, and inspected certain industrial areas in Siberia. The last three days of the visit abroad were spent in Poland. In response to remarks at a homecoming welcome in Washington by Acting Secretary of State Douglas Dillon, Nixon observed: "We have had a rather long journey. Sometimes it has been somewhat strenuous. It has never been dull."

Before leaving the Soviet Union, Vice President Nixon delivered an address broadcast over Moscow television and heard throughout the USSR by radio. This speech, delivered August 1, 1959, was reprinted, as agreed, in Soviet newspapers.

Vice President Nixon was nominated for the presidency at the Republican Convention in July 1960.

I first want to express my appreciation to the government of the USSR for giving me an opportunity to speak to the people of this country by radio and television just as Mr. Kozlov and Mr. Mikoyan spoke to the American people on their visits to my country.

[3] Text furnished by the Vice President, with permission to reprint.

[4] For biographical note, see Appendix; for references to earlier speeches, see Cumulative Author Index.

I realize that nine days is much too brief a time for a visitor to spend in this great country. But in that period I have had the opportunity of having extended and frank discussions with Mr. Khrushchev and other leaders of your government. I have visited Leningrad, Siberia and the Urals and I have had the privilege of meeting thousands of people in all walks of life.

What I would like to do tonight is to answer for the millions of people who are listening to this program some of the questions which were asked me over and over again on this trip so that you may get a true picture of the policies of the American government and people.

I should like to begin by answering a question which I often heard: What are my impressions of this country and its people?

While my visit was brief I did have a chance in addition to visiting this great capital city of Moscow to see the beauty and culture of Leningrad whose brave people won the admiration of the world for their heroic defense of their city during the war; to savor the inspiring pioneer spirit of Novosibirsk; to witness firsthand the thriving productivity of the factory complex of the Urals. I was greatly impressed by the efficient modern equipment of your factories; your magnificent ballets in Leningrad and Novosibirsk; by the competitive drive for progress which is evident on every side.

But most of all I was impressed by your people; after all, the greatest asset of a country is not its forests, its factories or its farms but its people.

These are some of the characteristics of the Soviet people which I particularly noted on this trip.

First, their capacity for hard work, their vitality; their intense desire to improve their lot, to get ahead, is evident everywhere.

There was another feature about the Soviet people which I noted that may surprise you and that is in how many respects you are like us Americans. We are similar in our love of humor —we laugh at the same jokes. The people of your frontier East have much the spirit of what was our frontier West.

We have a common love of sports; the name of Vasily Kuznetsov, your great decathlon champion, is known in the United States as well as it is in the Soviet Union. We are both a hospitable, friendly people. When we meet each other we tend to like each other personally, as so many of our soldiers who met during the last great war can attest.

Above all, the American people and the Soviet people are as one in their desire for peace. And our desire for peace is not because either of us is weak. On the contrary, each of us is strong and respects the strength the other possesses.

This means that if we are to have peace it must be a just peace based on mutual respect rather than the peace of surrender or dictation by either side. Putting it bluntly, both of our peoples want peace, but both of us also possess great strength and much as we want peace neither of us can or will tolerate being pushed around.

That is why I was so surprised at a question that was asked me by a worker on the new scientific center outside of Novosibirsk. My heart went out to him as he told me that he had been wounded in World War II and that his father and mother had been killed by bombs. But then he said, "I don't believe you when you say America is for peace."

Nothing he could have said could have astonished or saddened me more.

And so to the millions of Soviet people who suffered or lost their loved ones in war, and to all of those in this great country who want peace, I say tonight, if you doubt that the American Government and the American people are as dedicated to peace as you are, look at our record, examine our policies and you can reach only one conclusion—only aggressor nations have anything to fear from the United States of America.

We have fought in two world wars and have demanded and received not an acre of territory or a cent in reparations. We enjoy the highest standard of living of any people in the world's history, and there is nothing whatever that we want from any other people in the world except to live in peace and friendship with them. No leader in the world today could be more dedicated to peace than our President. As his brother, who has honored us by making this visit with us, can tell you, President Eisenhower's whole life is proof of the stark but simple truth—that no one hates war more than one who has seen a lot of it.

We know as do you that in this age of nuclear weapons it is impossible for either of our nations to launch an attack which would not bring terrible destruction to itself.

In this age any leader who is so insane even to think of starting a war should well heed your proverb—"Do not dig a pit for another; you may fall into it yourself."

Why then is there any doubt that the American government and people are just as dedicated to peace as the people of the USSR? I think part of the answer is to be found in another question which was often asked of me on this trip and which Mr. Khrushchev, himself, raised in this manner in his speech on July 28 at Dnepropetrovsk. "If you believe in the peaceful intentions of our country, why do you continue the arms race, why do you construct new military bases around our borders?"

In answering this question, let me first point out that these bases are not maintained for purposes of attacking you but for purposes of defending ourselves and our allies.

Why did we think it was necessary to set up bases? Let us look at the record. We disarmed rapidly after World War II. Then came a series of events which threatened our friends abroad as well as ourselves. The Berlin blockade and the war in Korea are typical of the actions which led the United States and our allies to rearm so that we could defend ourselves against aggression.

We must also remember that these events occurred before the Twentieth Party Congress changed the line to the one Mr. Khrushchev enunciated again in his speech at Dneprope-trovsk—that communism will now try to achieve its international objectives by peaceful means rather than by force. I could cite statement after statement made by previous leaders of the USSR which advocated and threatened the use of force against non-Communist countries in order to achieve Communist objectives.

A striking illustration of why we maintain bases and strong military forces is the fact that one fourth of the entire production of the USSR goes into armaments. This, in effect, means that every worker in the Soviet Union works one day out of four for armaments. And we in our country are also bearing a heavy burden of armaments. Think what it could mean to both of our countries if we could lift this burden from the backs of our people.

Some may ask, why don't we get rid of the bases since the Soviet Government declares today that it has only peaceful intentions? The answer is that whenever the fear and suspicion that caused us and our allies to take measures for collective self-defense are removed, the reason for our maintaining bases will be removed. In other words, the only possible solution of this problem lies in mutual rather than unilateral action leading toward disarmament.

Another question which was often asked was why won't the United States agree to stop the tests of atomic weapons? The answer in a nutshell is that the question is not whether we both should enter into an agreement to stop tests but whether that agreement is one which will make sure that the tests actually are stopped.

That is why we say that if both sides honestly want to stop tests, we must first agree to set up inspection procedures in both of our countries which will make certain that the agreement is not violated. We believe this position is the only one that gives assurance of accomplishing the objective of stopping tests rather than just signing an agreement to do so.

We are encouraged by the fact that at least in this area we are presently engaged in serious negotiations which have made some progress. I know that I express the sentiments of the people of both of our countries when I say that I am hopeful that these negotiations will finally end in agreement.

Another question that has often been asked me went something like this: "The United States says it is for peace, but what the world wants are deeds not words, and the United States is short on deeds and long on words."

Nothing could be further from the truth. It is possible that many of you listening to me are not aware of the positive programs the United States has proposed which were designed to contribute to peace. Let me tell you about just a few of them and what happened to them:

We had a monopoly on the atomic bomb when on June 14, 1946, we submitted the Baruch plan for international control of atomic energy. What happened? It was rejected by the USSR.

Under Article 43 of the United Nations Charter, provision was made for the establishment of the United Nations Armed Forces to keep the peace. On June 4, 1947, we made the first of many requests that agreement be reached. What happened? All have been rejected by the USSR.

At the Summit conference in Geneva on July 21, 1955, President Eisenhower made his offer of open skies aerial inspection. What happened? It was rejected by the USSR.

On May 1, 1958, the United States offered an Arctic aerial inspection plan to protect both nations from surprise attack. What happened? It was rejected by the USSR.

I realize that your government has indicated reasons for its rejection of each of these proposals. I do not list these proposals for the purpose of warming over past history but simply to demonstrate the initiative that our government has taken to reduce tensions and to find peaceful solutions for differences between us.

I realize that my answers to these questions indicate that there are some very basic differences between us. But let me emphasize at the same time that the very fact that we have not made as much progress as we would like in the past in settling our differences is the strongest reason for us to redouble our efforts to create better understanding between our two countries; to remove fear, suspicion and misconception where they exist, and thereby, to pave the way for discussions and eventual settlement by agreement of some of the basic conflicts between us.

We should both frankly recognize that we have some very real differences; that they are not easily settled: But two men who are friends can settle an argument between them without using their fists and two nations who want to be friends can do so without war.

I should like to suggest tonight some practical steps which will contribute to the cause of peace to which we are both dedicated.

First there are some positive things we can do which will create better understanding between us.

We can start by removing the language barrier. Here is one place where you are ahead of us. I was amazed at the number of people I met on this trip who were studying English. What we need are millions of American students who understand Russian and millions of Soviet students who understand English.

Both the exchange of persons and the cultural exchange programs should not only be continued but sharply expanded. The more Americans who visit and get to know first-hand the people of the Soviet Union and the more Soviet citizens who do the same in the United States, the better understanding we shall have.

I believe also that visits by officials like the ones Mr. Mikoyan and Mr. Kozlov made to the United States and which I have just concluded can provide the means of frank and full discussion of some of our problems and the development of solutions for them. Consequently, we should explore ways of increasing contacts of this type.

Most important of all, we need a much freer exchange of information between our two countries so that misconceptions we may have about you and that you have about us may be removed. I was rather surprised that Mr. Khrushchev should raise a question about the failure of the Western press to report adequately one of his recent statements. I would estimate that at least one hundred of Mr. Khrushchev's words are printed in our American press for every one word of President Eisenhower's speeches that are printed in the Soviet press.

Perhaps this is an area where the cause of better understanding would be served if we had a more equal exchange. Let us agree that all of Mr. Khrushchev's speeches on foreign policy be printed in the United States and that all of President Eisenhower's speeches on foreign policy be printed in the Soviet Union.

Why not go further and set up regular radio and television broadcasts by Mr. Khrushchev to the American people in return for President Eisenhower having the same privilege to talk to the Soviet people?

Let us put a stop to the jamming of broadcasts so that the Soviet people may hear broadcasts from our country just as the American people can hear forty hours of broadcasts a day from the Soviet Union. And let us have a freer flow of newspapers and magazines so that the Soviet people can buy American newspapers and magazines here just as we Americans purchased over one and a half million Soviet publications last year alone.

I recognize that freedom of information can be abused and that neither of us is free from blame in this respect. The press, radio, television and other means of communication such as film studios, have a heavy responsibility for maintaining the spirit of truth and for preventing misinformation. In the final analysis the misrepresentation of facts or distortion of the truth defeats itself. Let me give you an example from an experience that occurred to me on this trip.

There was a report in *Pravda* to the effect that on the morning after I arrived in Moscow I tried to give money to a poor Soviet citizen, with the hope that American press photographers might take pictures of the incident and send them around the world. There was not a shred of truth to this story.

Here is what actually happened. On an early morning visit to the Danilovsky Market, I had talked to scores of people and received a most friendly welcome. As I was about to leave, several of the people asked me for tickets to the American Exhibition. I told them I did not have any with me, but that I would be glad to buy some tickets for those present who wanted to attend the exhibition. One of the group explained that it was not a question of their not having money for the tickets, but simply a question of their not being able to obtain them. I told him I would be glad to check into the matter and see if I could get tickets for him.

These are the simple facts as far as this incident was concerned, and I can only add that all irresponsible reporters should never forget that in the end the truth always catches up with a lie.

Through this greater exchange of information between our two peoples we not only learn from each other and improve our way of life but we reduce the suspicion, the mistrust, the fear and misunderstanding and assure the understanding and friendship which will lead to the peace we all want. That is why, to me, the concept of co-existence is completely inadequate and negative. Co-existence implies that the world must be divided into two hostile camps with a wall of hate and fear between.

What we need today is not two worlds but one world where different peoples choose the economic and political systems which they want, but where there is free communication among all the peoples living on this earth.

Let us expand the concept of open skies. What the world also needs are open cities, open minds and open hearts.

Let us have peaceful competition not only in producing the best factories but in producing better lives for our people.

Let us cooperate in our exploration of outer space. As a worker told me in Novosibirsk, let us go to the moon together.

Let our aim be not victory over other peoples but the victory of all mankind over hunger, want, misery and disease, wherever it exists in the world.

I realize that this era of peaceful competition and even cooperation seems like an impossible dream when we consider the present differences we have between us. But the leaders of our countries can help make this dream come true. So far as the leader of our country is concerned, I can assure you that President Eisenhower has no objective to which he is more dedicated.

As far as Mr. Khrushchev is concerned, as I am sure you know, we disagree sharply on political and economic philosophy and on many world problems. But these characteristics are evident to anyone who meets him—He is a self-made man who worked his way up from the bottom; he is an articulate spokesman for the economic system in which he believes; he has immense drive;

in sum, he is one of those individuals who, whether you agree with him or disagree with him, is a born leader of men. Because he has these unique qualities and because the decisions he makes will affect not only the 200 million people of the USSR but the 3 billion people on this earth, he carries a tremendous responsibility on his shoulders.

I would not be so presumptuous as to try to give him advice on how he should fulfill that responsibility. But could I relate something that I noted on the trip I have just completed? In every factory and on hundreds of billboards I saw this slogan, "Let us work for the victory of communism."

If Mr. Khrushchev means by this slogan working for a better life for the people within the Soviet Union, that is one thing. If, on the other hand, he means the victory of communism over the United States and other countries, this is a horse of a different color. For we have our own ideas as to what system is best for us.

If he devotes his immense energies and talents to building a better life for the people of his own country, Mr. Khrushchev can go down in history as one of the greatest leaders the Soviet people have ever produced. But if he diverts the resources and talents of his people to the objective of promoting the communization of countries outside the Soviet Union, he will only assure that both he and his people will continue to live in an era of fear, suspicion, and tension.

The Geneva conference is a case in point. It would not be proper for me to comment on the specific proposals that are pending before that conference at this time. But agreements between great powers cannot be reached unless they take into account the views and interests of all parties concerned. I was encouraged to note in my conversations with Mr. Khrushchev that he recognizes this fact and agrees that a successful outcome of this conference could be a great step forward in settling some of the problems I have discussed tonight.

I have one final thought to add. Mr. Khrushchev predicted that our grandchildren would live under communism. He reiterated this to me in our talks last Sunday.

Let me say that we do not object to his saying this will happen. We only object if he tries to bring it about.

And this is my answer to him. I do not say that your grandchildren will live under capitalism. We prefer our system. But the very essence of our belief is that we do not and will not try to impose our system on anybody else. We believe that you and all other peoples on this earth should have the right to choose the kind of economic or political system which best fits your particular problems without any foreign intervention.

As I leave your country, I shall never forget an incident that occurred as I was driving through your beautiful Ural Mountains. A group of children on the side of the road threw wild flowers into my car and cried in English the words "friendship," "friendship." Mr. Zhukov told me that the first word children who study English are taught is the word "friendship." There could be no more eloquent expression of the attitude of the Soviet people, an attitude which we share in common with you.

Finally, may I express on behalf of my wife and I, and all the members of our party, our deep appreciation for the warm friendship and boundless hospitality we have found everywhere we have gone in the Soviet Union. I pledge to you that in the years to come I shall devote my best efforts to the cause of peace with justice for all the peoples of the world.

"PEACE AND FRIENDSHIP, IN FREEDOM" [5]

Dwight D. Eisenhower [6]

Grand tours were in diplomatic vogue in 1959. In early November, President Eisenhower announced that he would soon depart on a journey to three continents, for a total of over 22,000 miles—clearly the longest trip ever undertaken by a President in office. Other goodwill tours of no inconsiderable distances were planned for 1960: a trip to Latin America in late February, a return visit to Premier Khrushchev (which failed to come off because of the Summit fiasco), and a journey to the Far East in June.

On the evening of December 3, 1959, the President left for Rome —the first stop on the route that eventually took him to Ankara, Karachi, New Delhi, and Athens, among other places. Just a few moments before departure, he addressed the nation over television and radio. Obviously he was intent upon giving more than a farewell speech. He used the occasion to point up national urgencies: the necessity for early settlement of the steel dispute and the resolve to maintain military strength adequate for security "until the conference table can replace the battlefield as the arbiter of world affairs."

The speech sounded other grave notes. At the end of the President's journey on December 19, the Big Four (Eisenhower, Macmillan, de Gaulle, and Adenauer) would have to deal with some thorny diplomatic issues, growing in part out of France's seeming inclination toward greater independence from NATO and of certain differences among the Western powers on how best to deal with the Russians.

Even if by indirection, the President's speech was somewhat of a prelude to the East-West Summit meeting, which ended before it began in mid-May. It seemed to say that the "spirit of Camp David" would soon face a stern test. "We have heard much of the phrase, 'Peace and Friendship,'" said the President near the close of his address. "This phrase, in expressing the aspirations of America, is not complete. We should say instead, 'Peace and Friendship, in Freedom.'"

Good evening fellow Americans—

I leave, in just a few minutes, on a three-week journey half way around the world. During this mission of peace and good

[5] Text "as actually delivered" furnished by Mrs. Anne Wheaton, associate press secretary to the President, with permission for this reprint.

[6] For biographical note, see Appendix; for references to earlier speeches see Cumulative Author Index.

will I hope to promote a better understanding of America and to learn more of our friends abroad.

In every country I hope to make widely known America's deepest desire—a world in which all nations may prosper in freedom, justice, and peace, unmolested and unafraid.

I shall try to convey to everyone our earnestness in striving to reduce the tensions dividing mankind—an effort first requiring, as indeed Mr. Khrushchev agrees, the beginning of mutual disarmament. Of course, I shall stress that the first requirement for mutual disarmament is mutual verification.

Then I hope to make this truth clear—that, on all this earth, not anywhere does our nation seek territory, selfish gain or unfair advantage for itself. I hope all can understand that beyond her shores, as at home, America aspires only to promote human happiness, justly achieved.

We in America know that for many decades our nation has practiced and proclaimed these convictions and purposes. But this is not enough. For years doubts about us have been skillfully nurtured in foreign lands by those who oppose America's ideals.

Our country has been unjustly described as one pursuing only materialistic goals; as building a culture whose hallmarks are gadgets and shallow pleasures; as prizing wealth above ideals, machines above spirit, leisure above learning, and war above peace.

Actually, as our Declaration proclaims, the core of our nation is belief in a Creator who has endowed all men with inalienable rights, including life, liberty and the pursuit of happiness. In that belief is our country's true hallmark—a faith that permeates every aspect of our political, social and family life. This truth, too, I hope to emphasize abroad.

Of course, as all the world knows, at times, and in some respects, we have fallen short of the high ideals held up for us by our founding fathers. But one of the glories of America is that she never ceases her striving toward the shining goal.

And in this striving, we know we still can learn much from other cultures. From the ideals and achievements of others, we can gain new inspiration. We do not forget that, in the eyes of millions in older lands, our America is still young—in some respects, is still on trial.

So I earnestly make this suggestion, as I start this journey tonight—that you, and those close to you, join with me in a renewed dedication to our moral and spiritual convictions, and in that light re-examine our own record, including our shortcomings. May this examination inspire each of us so to think and so to act, as to hasten our progress toward the goals our fathers established, which have made America an instrument for good. In this rededication we shall replenish the true source of America's strength—her faith; and, flowing from it, her love of liberty, her devotion to justice.

So believing, we look on our nation's great wealth as more than a hard earned resource to be used only for our own material good. We believe that it should also serve the common good, abroad as well as at home. This is not sheer altruism. If we can truly cooperate with other nations—especially our friends of the free world—we can, first defeat the evils of hunger, privation and disease that throughout the ages have plagued mankind. Thus we can develop a healthier, more prosperous world, and in the process develop greater prosperity for ourselves. Even more than this, we can help reduce the world tensions that are the powder kegs of disaster.

This is why, for more than a decade, America has engaged in cooperative programs with other nations—programs that, in many ways, concern the areas that I set forth to visit tonight. Our part of this effort is our own "Mutual Security Program." Abroad, it is supplemented and its effects many times multiplied by programs of all the countries associated with us in this work.

Thus we provide a peaceful barrier, erected by freedom, to the continuous probings of predatory force. Our mutual undertakings support those who strive to forestall aggression, subversion and penetration. It helps steady the struggling economies of free nations new and old. It helps build strength and hope, preventing collapse and despair. In a world sorely troubled by an atheistic imperialism, it is a strong instrument of hope and of encouragement to others who are eager, with us, to do their part in sustaining the human spirit and human progress.

So we see that our nation's security, economic health, and hope for peace demand of all of us a continuing support of these cooperative efforts, initiated a dozen years ago. Of the amounts we devote to our own security and to peace, none yields a more beneficial return than the dollars we apply to these mutual efforts of the free world.

Here at home, we are fortunate in having an economy so richly productive as to sustain a most powerful defense without impairment of human values. Without this military strength our efforts to provide a shield for freedom and to preserve and strengthen peace would be futile. We are determined that in a quality and power this force shall forever be kept adequate for our security needs until the conference table can replace the battlefield as the arbiter of world affairs.

This kind of defense is costly and burdensome, as indeed are many other essential Federal programs. For example, the annual interest alone, on our Federal debt, is now more than nine billion dollars a year—a sum in dollars equal to the entire Federal budget of 1940. We must, then, for our security and our prosperity, keep our economy vigorous and expanding. We can keep it so, but only if we meet wisely and responsibly the economic problems that confront us. To mention a few, there are inflation, public spending, taxation, production costs and foreign trade, agriculture, and labor-management relations.

Of these problems, one cries out for immediate solution. I refer to the labor-management dispute that is still unresolved in the steel industry.

This, I am sure, is clear to us all: the success of all our efforts to build and sustain the peace depends not only upon our spiritual and military strength, but also upon the health of our economy. Among sovereign nations progress toward a just peace can be achieved only through international cooperation. Likewise, economic strength, in this nation of free citizens, requires cooperation among us all. We cannot—any of us—

indulge our own desires, our own demands, our own emotions, to the extent of working hardship throughout the country.

"Responsible citizenship" in a free country means what it says. It means conducting oneself responsibly, in the interest of others as well as self. America will not—indeed, it cannot—tolerate for long the crippling of the entire economy as the result of labor-management disputes in any one basic industry or any group of industries.

Among our free people there is no one man, no one group, no one industry, no one interest, that measures, in importance, to America.

So, my friends, the choice is up to free American employers and American employees. Voluntarily, in the spirit of free collective bargaining, they will act responsibly; or else, in due course their countrymen will see to it that they do act responsibly. It is up to labor and management, in these disputes, to adjust responsibly and equitably their differences. The nation is determined to preserve free enterprise, including free collective bargaining. It we are to do this, labor and management alike must see to it, in every dispute and settlement, that the public interest is as carefully protected as the interests of stockholders and of employees. The public will not stand for less.

Tonight, despite months of effort, labor and management in the steel industry are still in disagreement. As I leave tonight, America still faces the possibility of a renewed steel crisis, beginning a few weeks hence.

Day after day, throughout the economy, uncertainty, indecision and hesitation are growing as a result of this continuing controversy. Now, negotiations have just been resumed. The exact methods the parties agree upon to advance these negotiations are of relatively little importance to the American people. The leaders of both segments must realize that the achievement of a voluntary settlement, fair to all, is critically important to the entire nation. Indeed, it is so important that I am instructing the director of the mediation and conciliation service to do all that he can to keep the parties negotiating on an around-the-clock basis.

America needs a settlement now.

During these next three weeks, while I am talking of peace and of mutual cooperation with our friends abroad, the subject of America's spiritual and economic strength is bound to come up often and importantly. What great news it would be if, during the course of this journey, I should receive word of a settlement of this steel controversy that is fair to the workers, fair to management, and above all, fair to the American people.

One last thought. We have heard much of the phrase, "Peace and Friendship." This phrase, in expressing the aspirations of America, is not complete. We should say instead, "Peace and Friendship, in Freedom." This, I think, is America's real message to the world.

Now, my friends, I set forth as your agent to extend once again to millions of people across the seas assurance of America's sincere friendship. I know you wish me well. And, I wish you well in making your influence felt, individually and collectively, in solving, properly, our pressing problems here at home. For let us remember—these two efforts—the one abroad and the one at home—actually are one and inseparable. Working cooperatively together, here at home, rather than wasting our effort and substance in bitter economic and political strife, we in America will become ever a stronger force on the side of good in the world.

And, as we, through our cooperative efforts abroad, strengthen human understanding and good will throughout the world, we bring ever closer the day of lasting peace.

May the Almighty inspire us all, in these efforts, to do our best.

Good night, and for three weeks, good-bye.

DEDICATIONS TO STRENGTH AND GREATNESS

INDEPENDENCE DAY ADDRESS [1]

Ernest Gruening [2]

"So the bill was passed." The words were those of the late Senator Richard Neuberger, presiding officer at the moment. The "simple finality of those five words," said Senator Ernest Gruening (Democrat, Alaska), were "to me the real climax of this American drama" which ended on June 30, 1958, when Congress voted statehood for Alaska. President Eisenhower signed the formal document of proclamation on January 3, 1959, and ordered the addition of the forty-ninth star to the flag, effective July 4. The flag bearing the additional star was presented for the first time to the city of Philadelphia on July 4 by Senator Hugh D. Scott of Pennsylvania.

"We are celebrating the admission to the Union of the largest state in American history.

"We are celebrating the admission of an area larger than it ever before admitted to the Union in any one year—an area one-fifth as large as the older forty-eight states."

These words appear in Senator Gruening's address in which he memorializes this exciting event in American history. The address was given at Independence Hall, Philadelphia, on July 4, 1959.

It is a rare privilege that you have accorded me in asking me to address you on this occasion, or, perhaps, to use the English language more precisely, a unique privilege.

For this is no ordinary Fourth of July.

This is an Independence Day ceremony which, in several important respects, is unprecedented—and therefore, unique.

We are celebrating the admission to the Union of the largest state in American history.

We are celebrating the admission of an area larger than it ever before admitted to the Union in any one year—an area one-fifth as large as the older forty-eight states.

---

[1] Text from the *Congressional Record*. 105:A5811-13. Jl. 7, '59. Reprinted by permission of Senator Gruening.
[2] For biographical note, see Appendix.

We are celebrating the admission to the Union of a state that extends American dominion and full citizenship, and all concomitant blessings that American citizenship implies, to America's farthest west and America's farthest north.

Thus, we are celebrating the extension, for the first time in history, of the Union north into the Arctic and west into the Eastern Hemisphere. This is new terrain for the family of states.

We are celebrating the admission to the Union, for the first time, of a non-contiguous area—this is the first time that we have taken into the family of states territory which did not touch the rectangular block that hitherto has constituted the Union.

We are celebrating the admission of a new state after forty-six years without such evidence of growth and expansion. Thirteen years was previously the longest interval between the admission of states.

These geographical and historical data imply a great deal more than their mere recital reveals. Behind these physical facts lie far more important symbolic and spiritual connotations. These are, first, that the United States is not static, not limited, not complete; but, on the contrary, is dynamic, growing, and on the march.

How significant is this?

It is true that throughout our history the voices of doubt and pessimism about the future of our Republic have been raised.

It would surprise many of you to know that the prophets of gloom and doom were heard almost as soon as our nation was founded. History has repeatedly proven them completely mistaken.

In the last two years, alarm has been expressed—especially since the Russian achievements in outer space—that the United States had reached its peak of power and influence. In not a few places was the fear voiced that despite our great material achievements, our position of eminence in the world, our vast resources, our proved potentials and capabilities, our pioneering and leadership in many fields, all these had reached a climax and an apex from which recession would before long begin.

Comparisons have been made with ancient Rome, which, while apparently at the zenith of its imperial power and glory, was being insidiously corroded within by luxury and sybaritic living, and was shortly to succumb to the onslaught of the cruder and tougher barbarians. Parallels have been latterly drawn to forecast that similarly, our luxurious, high standards of American living, and a consequent softness which this way of life presumably predicates, will cause us ere long to succumb to the ruthless aggressiveness of the hordes, mobilized by the governments in Moscow and Peiping—hordes unused to the refinements of Western civilization.

While it is well never to underrate one's opponents—and it is clear that at the present times the enemies of our freedom and of the whole free world lie in the rulerships of the totalitarian Communist police states—I boldly assert my conviction that the event that we are particularly celebrating today furnishes a substantial refutation of the apprehension that Uncle Sam is shortly to begin to dodder and to enter dotage.

Within the short space of one year, the United States has admitted the forty-ninth and fiftieth states—Alaska and Hawaii. And while technically, Hawaii is not yet in the Union, and while officially, the new Old Glory we are unfurling here today signalizes the admission only of the forty-ninth state—Alaska—we would be remiss in not hailing this double achievement.

For while Alaska's admission extends the frontiers of democracy to America's farthest North and farthest West, Hawaii's admission extends them to America's farthest South.

While Alaska's admission extends America into the Arctic, Hawaii's admission extends it into the tropics.

The Union's boundaries a year ago extended between approximately the 67th meridian and 125th meridian of longitude west and the parallels of approximately 25 degrees north latitude and 49 degrees north latitude. Now, they extend between approximately 67 degrees west longitude and 173 degrees east longitude and the parallels of approximately 19 degrees north to 73 degrees north latitude.

But the geographical extension is not the significant aspect of these achievements. The totalitarian police states have likewise enlarged their dominion. Within the lifetime of many living, we have seen the rulers of the Kremlin extend their brutal tyranny over a dozen formerly free and independent nations. Within a few weeks, we have seen the masters of Peiping invade and conquer the formerly free land of Tibet.

In contrast, the United States has to its new states extended that most basic of American principles—the principle of government by consent of the governed. What a contrast between Uncle Sam's treatment of his former dependencies—which is what Alaska and Hawaii, under territorial status, have been— and the Russian treatment of Hungary and the Chinese treatment of Tibet.

There is a special significance in our two extensions. Alaska was formerly Russian-America; and but for the wisdom and vision of William H. Seward, Secretary of State in President Lincoln's and President Johnson's Cabinets, Alaska might still be groaning under the Kremlin's heel.

We can stand today on the shores of the Alaskan mainland and look across the Bering Strait and see the headlands of Siberia. Only fifty-four miles separate these two areas; but what a world of contrast in the lives of their peoples.

In the Bering Sea are two islands, only two and one-half miles apart—the Diomedes. The international dateline passes between them. Little Diomede is American; Big Diomede is Russian. A couple of decades ago, these two islands were sparsely inhabited by Eskimos. They visited freely, paddling across the narrow Strait between them in the summertime in kayaks or oomiaks—the two varieties of native skinboats—or crossing over on the ice bridge which furnished a passageway between them for eight months of the year. When the Iron Curtain descended upon Russia, the Soviet authorities evacuated their Eskimos, uprooted them from where they had lived, and removed them to the mainland of Siberia. The Eskimos of Little

Diomede, on the other hand, were proud to enroll themselves as volunteers in the Alaska Territorial Guard during World War II, and eager thereafter to serve their territory, and now state and nation, as members of the Alaska National Guard. History and geography furnish here, on the northwestern edge of our continent, the great contrast between the two systems, theirs and ours.

In Hawaii, our fiftieth state, you will find a meeting of East and West. There, united in the common ideology that is America's proudest heritage—the heritage of individual liberty, of freedom of speech, press, assembly, and worship, that are guaranteed us by the Bill of Rights—is the finest example of ethnic democracy to be found not only under the American flag, but anywhere on earth. There, the races of East and West have mingled. To the Polynesian inhabitants whom the early explorers found there at the very end of the eighteenth century came the New England missionaries, and uniting with the aboriginal inhabitants, created a culture that is beautifully diverse in its outer aspects, but completely saturated with the principles of democracy.

To these islands came people from the Orient—from China, from Japan, from Korea, from the Philippines—who, as citizens of the fiftieth state, will constitute a bridge between East and West, contrary to Rudyard Kipling's pronouncement that East and West will never meet. They have met here, they will continue to meet here, under the flag which we are raising today, and which, a year from today, will display its fiftieth star.

Now, the inclusion of the forty-ninth and fiftieth stars today, and a year from today, demonstrate the most striking and unique fact about the American flag. It is the only flag which grows with the growth of the nation. While its basic design remains unchanged, it does change just sufficiently in one recurring detail to record the amazing growth from a thin fringe of colonies along the Atlantic seaboard to the mighty nation that the United States has become.

Indeed, each additional star represents a verse in the American epic, and it is appropriate, on this occasion, when a new star has been added, to emphasize that point and bring out the close relationship between the American flag and the Union whose emblem it is.

As we all know, our flag received its design 182 years ago from the Continental Congress. The Congress properly decided that the thirteen colonies which had banded together to form our nation should be represented both by the alternating red and white stripes and by the thirteen stars in the canton or union of the flag. For a time, it was assumed that each new state would be recorded by an additional star and additional stripe, and when our first two states were admitted—Vermont and Kentucky, in 1791 and 1792, respectively—our flag had fifteen stars and fifteen stripes.

But Congress soon realized that an additional star in the blue firmament provided adequate recognition for a new state; that likewise adding a new stripe for each state would not only entail needless duplication, but would, in time, diminish the beauty of design of the flag by overburdening it with stripes. Likewise, this duplication would destroy the great historic symbolism inherent in the memory of the original thirteen colonies and the original thirteen states. Therefore, 141 years ago, the Congress returned to its original formula, which persists to this day—namely, thirteen stripes forever, and an additional star for each new state.

Thirty-seven stars have been added to the original thirteen. But that does not mean that our flagmakers have had to make thirty-seven different flags and thirty-seven times scrap those on hand. A sufficient number of states came in at one time so that changes had to be made, or will have to be made, only about twenty-seven times instead of thirty-seven. No historical museum could collect more than twenty-seven different American flags because they do not exist.

In the nearly three-quarters of a century between the formation of the Union and the Civil War, not a few states came in in pairs. The dates of their admission did not coincide exactly, but their joint entry into statehood was prearranged, and by design.

Each star that has been added to our flag represents a stirring chapter in our history, each new star signalized a step in the progress of mankind. Each star incarnates a portion of the hopes, the struggles, the trials and errors, the quest for goals, and the achievements that together constitute the American saga.

It is, I believe, the greatest epic of all time. It is the greatest epic because it stories the untrammeled efforts of freemen—freer than any of their predecessors in the pageant of history—to work out their own destiny.

So we must not think of our flag only as an emblem. We must not think of it merely as a symbol, though of course it is very much a symbol—a symbol of everything that our American faith embodies. But we should think of it also as a symposium of great adventures—adventures of mind and heart and body—a recording of past performance, proudly raised on high for each coming generation to look up to, ever a summons to present obligation and a guide to future conduct.

We cannot identify any one of the thirteen stripes with any one of the original thirteen states. We might have done so—or might do so—if someone wished arbitrarily to relate each stripe from the top of the flag down to each state in the chronological order of its adherence to the Union. That would assign to Delaware, our oldest state, the topmost stripe. It would award to Pennsylvania the second stripe from the top. Rhode Island's would be the stripe at the lower edge of the flag since it was the thirteenth state to sign up.

It was wholly appropriate that Delaware, the first state to enter the Union, should adopt as its motto, "Liberty and Independence." Perhaps this is the time and place to advert to the fact that Pennsylvania, which decided to enter the Union five days after Delaware, amplified Delaware's ringing words "Liberty and Independence" by preceding them with the word "virtue," so that as you all know, the Keystone state's motto is: "Virtue, Liberty and Independence." Possibly the five-day interval between Delaware's signing of the Constitution on December 7, 1787, and Pennsylvania's adherence on December 12, led Benjamin Franklin and his colleagues in the Pennsylvania delegation to reflect that they already had liberty and independence and needed to prescribe virtue additionally to safeguard and amplify the blessings of their new-found freedom. It might be worth mentioning that the motto of the third state to ratify, six days after Pennsylvania—New Jersey—was "Liberty and Prosperity." Thus was perhaps illustrated the rapidity of progress in our national infancy—all in the course of eleven days—from the newly achieved "Liberty and Independence" hailed by Delaware, to the addition of "virtue" by Pennsylvania, and the substitution by New Jersey for Pennsylvania's somewhat austere prescription of "virtue," the less arduous and perhaps more alluring goal of "prosperity."

Incidentally, those three first states—Delaware, your own State of Pennsylvania, and New Jersey—all contiguous to each other, were the only states to join the Union in 1787. Not until after the New Year, 1788, had begun, did the others follow. Here in the very heart of the new-born Republic, midway between New Hampshire to the north and Georgia, to the south, were the pioneer states, the first three to pledge their allegiance to the Constitution and flag of the United States.

I wonder that no one has thought to form an inner club, an exclusive order within some of the sons and daughters of yesteryear, entitling it: "The Joiners of 1787." Something analogous to it occurred a century later in Alaska. There, in what Alaskans fondly call the last frontier, "pioneering," a beloved word, dates from the days of '98 romantically eternalized in the verse of Robert W. Service and the short stories of Jack London. 'Ninety-eight was the year of the great gold rush that followed the discovery of gold in the Klondike. No candidate for public office in Alaska fails to claim—if he can truthfully do so—that he was a '98 pioneer. But several years ago, a charming lady, a candidate for Alaska's Territorial House of Representatives, proclaimed in her political advertisements that she was an '87 pioneer. She had been carried across the Chilkoot Pass in that year as a babe in arms, eleven years before the

Klondike. She did not want to be mistaken for any of the Johnny-come-latelys of '98. She was elected.

It would perhaps be painting the lily to pursue further the theme of the rapid progressiveness of the sentiments in the subsequently enrolling states' mottoes, but it may be worth noting that Georgia, the fourth state, which came in on January 2, 1788, apparently considered "Liberty and Independence" now achieved, no longer timely, and instead looked to the future with the motto: "Wisdom, Justice, Moderation." May "The Empire State of the South" achieve them. They are desirable goals for any state.

If it is not customary to associate any one of the thirteen stripes in our flag with any of the original thirteen states, it is even more impossible to attach any one of the forty-nine stars to a given state. Yet we might well view the addition of each star to our flag as much more than a minor and automatic change on a piece of bunting. Rather, we should think of what lay behind that star, what preceded the admission of the new state that star represents, hail it as we would a great new star in the heavens, and reflect on the cosmic forces that brought it into being.

Who can relive the story of Vermont's gallant struggle for self-determination which culminated in its entering the Union as the fourteenth state—the first additional star in the flag—without sensing that the Green Mountain boys were reenacting on the home ground our own epoch-making revolution? From the outbreak of the War of Independence, Vermont was master of its destiny and determined to remain so. In those four years, between 1787 and 1791, Vermont had not had territorial status. It had steadfastly maintained its independence against the claims of adequate New Hampshire and of powerful New York, which Vermonters were prepared to resist, if need be, by arms. Likewise, Vermont rejected the tendered blandishment of union with Canada. It would join our Union, but only as an equal, as a sovereign state.

And now, early in our history, we come to the first of those interesting arrangements in which sectional balancing played a great part. For while Vermont was resisting the claims of two already established states, pioneers settled across the Appalachians in land belonging to Virginia, were trying similarly to free themselves from the grasp of Old Dominion, then by far the most populous—and by that token the most powerful—of all the thirteen states. There had been not fewer than ten conventions of representatives from Virginia and from the embryonic state of Kentucky in a vain effort to reach a solution. Finally, in 1791, under the leadership of Thomas Jefferson, a provision which satisfied conflicting claims and regional rivalry was achieved for the admission of both states, Vermont and Kentucky. This solution was reflected in a bit of doggerel which originated in a Pennsylvania newspaper and was widely reprinted in the press of that period:

> Kentucky to the Union given,
> Vermont will make the balance even;
> Still Pennsylvania holds the scales
> And neither South nor North prevails.

Thus, those first two new stars in the flag—the fourteenth and fifteenth—marked not only the advent of two states, but, with the admission of Kentucky, the beginning of the westward march that has so profoundly shaped the American character and contributed such unique quality to our American life.

The next three states—Tennessee in 1796, Ohio in 1803, and Louisiana in 1812—were admitted separately, but widely varying and unprecedented conditions accompanied the admission of each. The frontiersmen occupying the region south of Kentucky, and belonging to North Carolina, as I have pointed out, impatient at the delay in granting them admission to the Union, first set up a state of their own and called it Franklin, honoring your greatest Pennsylvanian. But receiving no invitation to join the Union from the first three Congresses, they assumed the initiative, drafted a constitution for the future state of Tennessee, elected two senators, and sent them here to knock at the door of Congress for admission. They were successful. In a few months, in 1796, Tennessee became the third new state.

With Ohio, represented by the seventeenth star, the frontier advanced across the Alleghenies north as well as south, ushering in the birth of that great American region known—perhaps not too exactly—as the Middle West. In Ohio, also, Virginia acquired a rival mother of presidents.

Before the next state, Louisiana, added the eighteenth star to our flag, President Jefferson's Louisiana Purchase had doubled the extent of American territory, and extended its western border to the Rockies.

Now there was a return to sectional balancing into which the issue of free versus slave states had crept, with the admission in 1816 of Indiana and in 1817 of Mississippi, represented by the nineteenth and twentieth stars.

The same pattern was followed shortly thereafter by the admission of Illinois in 1818 and Alabama in 1819, our twenty-first and twenty-second stars.

By now, the slavery issue in relation to the admission of new states had become more acute and led to the Missouri Compromise—an important milestone in our history, dealing with problems happily no longer existing. By it, Maine was admitted as a free state in 1820, our twenty-third star, and Missouri, our twenty-fourth star, in 1821 as a slave state but with certain limitations, while thereafter all future states west of the Mississippi River and north of 36°30′ were pledged to freedom.

Thereafter the free versus slave state issue would, for a time, dominate every new state's admission. Arkansas, a slave state, came in in 1836, Michigan, its offset, a free state, in 1837—our twenty-fifth and twenty-sixth stars—and following the same pattern, Florida in 1845 and Iowa in 1846, our twenty-seventh and twenty-ninth stars. For in between, Texas, in 1845, under unprecedented and dramatic circumstances, following its victorious war of independence, had come into the Union, bringing its own Lone Star with it, and, surprisingly, not insisting that when added to our flag that star should be bigger than all the rest, but reserving the right to divide itself into five states. Alaskans have been waiting breathlessly to see whether Texas will do it.

By this time, the irrepressible conflict was looming larger and the balancing in the admission of northern and southern states ceased. Texas was the last slave state admitted. Wisconsin placed the thirtieth star in the flag in 1848.

California, having loosened its bonds from Mexico, set up its own republic, was briefly under U.S. military rule, and scorning even a temporary condition of territorialism, was admitted to the Union in 1850. Its star—the thirty-first—marked the extension of American dominion to the Pacific.

Minnesota came next in 1858, followed by Oregon in 1859 and Kansas in 1861, respectively the thirty-second, thirty-third, and thirty-fourth stars in the flag.

The next two states were war babies. They were the direct consequences of the Civil War. When Virginia seceded in 1861, the state's forty western counties voted to remain loyal to the Union, rejected the action taken at Richmond, and set up an independent state with the capital at Wheeling, West Virginia, as these secessionists from secession called it, which was admitted to the Union in 1863. Probably no state was born under more stirring circumstances than was this neighbor of yours to the south and west. Its motto—Montani Semper Liberi (Mountaineers Always Free) both renews the aspiration for freedom voiced in the days of our War for Independence and reveals that West Virginia has the highest average altitude of any state east of the Rockies.

Nevada was brought into the Union in 1864 by President Lincoln to help him secure ratification of the thirteenth amendment to the Constitution which abolished slavery. Perhaps we might, with poetic license, call these two—the thirty-fifth and thirty-sixth stars—"Shooting Stars." They came into the Union amid the booming of cannon on the farflung battlefields, and as a direct consequence of that bloody family quarrel.

Nebraska followed in 1867, and Colorado in 1876. Dakota Territory was divided into two states in 1889, and in the same year Montana and Washington came into the Union. Idaho and Wyoming followed the next year, 1890. Six states in two years. Utah was added in 1896; Oklahoma in 1907, and the last two states, up to this time—New Mexico and Arizona—in 1912, brought the field of blue to yesterday's galaxy of forty-eight stars.

Now, a few concluding words about our forty-ninth and fiftieth states and stars.

William H. Seward, who was really the author of Alaska's entry into the United States, had a great vision of extending the American idea all over this continent. It was not mere territorial acquisition that concerned him. Into the Treaty of Cession he wrote:

> The inhabitants of the ceded territory shall be admitted to the enjoyment of all the rights, advantages, and immunities of the citizens of the United States.

Decades later, we Alaskans held up this statement before the Congress as a solemn pledge and promise. We argued—and, I am convinced, logically—that only by statehood could the inhabitants of Alaska be admitted to the enjoyment of all the rights, advantages, and immunities of citizens of the United States. Actually, as a territory, Alaska suffered an indifference, a neglect, and downright discrimination by the Federal Government which led to an increasing determination on the part of these frontiersmen of Alaska to achieve the full equality of statehood.

The first Alaska statehood bill was introduced in 1916 by James Wickersham, one of our early delegates, for, as a territory, Alaska could be represented in the Congress by only a voteless delegate in the House of Representatives. Of course, the bill did not even get out of committee. In the early 1940's, statehood bills were again introduced in the House by the then delegate, Anthony J. Dimond, and in the Senate by Senator William Langer, of North Dakota, and Senator Pat McCarran, of Nevada. These bills likewise did not get out of committee. In 1945, I had the opportunity to present to the Alaska Territorial Legislature a recommendation for a bill providing for a referendum in the coming election to determine officially the wishes of the people of Alaska concerning statehood. The legislation was adopted, and at the 1946 election, the people of Alaska voted that they wanted statehood. That was the begining of our present drive. President Truman enthusiastically endorsed statehood—the first President to do so—recommending, in his first state of the Union message in 1946, enabling legislation to the Congress, even before the vote of the people of Alaska had been recorded. Thereafter, our voteless delegate in the House introduced a statehood bill in every session of Congress. It was passed by the House in one session, but failed on action in the Senate. Meanwhile, we were all working to mobilize public sentiment, which soon ran way ahead of congressional action.

In 1955, the Alaska Legislature, impatient at the delays, decided on bold action. It passed an act providing for a constitutional convention which would draft a constitution for the state of Alaska, and appropriated $300,000 for that purpose, scorning the advice of the timid and prudent that if Alaska waited until Congress acted, the Federal Government would pay the cost of this convention. A speedy election for delegates followed, and they were elected on a nonpartisan basis. Fifty-five delegates —the same historic number that met here in Philadelphia in 1787 to draft the Constitution of the United States—met at the University of Alaska near Fairbanks in 1955, and drafted a constitution which political scientists declare to be at least the equal of any existing state charter. The people ratified it at the next election. They went further. At this same election they approved an ordinance which authorized the people of Alaska to nominate and elect two U.S. senators and a representative and send them to Washington to work for statehood. In doing this, we were following an ancient, but generally forgotten, precedent. In 1796, the people living west of the Appalachians and south of Kentucky, which then belonged to the state of North Carolina, were becoming impatient because the first three Congresses did not admit their area to statehood. They drew up a constitution and elected two senators, and sent them to the national capital—which was then Philadelphia—to work for statehood. They were successful. We therefore called our procedure the Alaska-Tennessee plan, after its originators, the pioneer mountaineers of Tennessee. A similar procedure was followed by Michigan, by Iowa, by California, by Minnesota, by Oregon, and by Kansas. Similarly, three of us were elected by

Alaskans. We went to Washington and were successful in persuading a majority of the members of both houses of Congress to pass a statehood bill in the Eighty-fifth Congress.

And once the ice had been broken, figuratively speaking, it was not difficult to bring in the last of the incorporated territories—our sister in the Pacific, Hawaii. In all fairness, it should be said that Hawaii was ready for statehood long before Alaska—it had met the basic tests earlier and should have been admitted before Alaska. But Alaskans were happy and proud to play an active part in bringing in the fiftieth state. We worked just as hard to bring in Hawaii as we had to bring in Alaska.

But I will leave the telling of Hawaii's gallant struggle to whoever succeeds me on this occasion a year hence.

However, you will see, from what I have said, that there is a great story behind the placement of each new star in our flag. Each star is a condensation of that story. Each, while different, is a saga of aspiration and effort, of sacrifice and struggle—all primarily for one basic purpose—the application of that principle proclaimed in the Declaration of Independence that governments derive their just powers from the consent of the governed. It was proclaimed as an unalienable right in this city in the Declaration of Independence. It guided our forefathers in the founding of the republic. It has guided all of us to national greatness.

As I pointed out earlier, in one respect our flag is unique. While it is one of the oldest national emblems on earth—older than any other in the New World and out-aged by very few in the old—it is the only flag which, while unaltered in basic design, yet changes progressively. It is the only flag which is not static. It records the birth of our nation; it codifies the nation's growth from infancy to maturity.

So, I would say to any of those who, in moods of depression or doubt, fear that our great civilization is in danger of decline, atrophy or decay, they can find in the flag not merely the inspiration, but the visible and tangible proof that America, the land which we love, and the idea that we cherish, is secure. As the forty-nine stars are unfurled in the breeze, we can lift our eyes and our hearts in the confident knowledge that the best is yet to come.

ALOHA KE AKUA [3]

ABRAHAM KAHIKINA AKAKA [4]

Word that Congress had granted statehood to Hawaii reached Honolulu just as the Reverend Abraham K. Akaka was offering a prayer before the Territorial Legislature assembled in Iolani Palace.

At ten on the following morning, territorial officials, legislators, and other citizens passed in solemn procession from the palace to Kawaiahao Church across the square. There, on the very spot where Christian missionaries had preached their first sermon, where kings and chief executives had repaired after assuming responsibilities of state, and where the people had prayed and sought encouragement in times of emergency and strife, an impressive service was conducted.

Outstanding in this ceremony was the sermon delivered by the Reverend Akaka. So graciously did he express the emotions and thoughts that passed through the hearts and minds of the people of Hawaii upon achieving the goal toward which they had struggled for so long, that thousands besieged him for copies of his words.[5]

These remarks are by Thomas Nickerson of the University of Hawaii Press from the foreword to the text of Reverend Akaka's sermon, published by the University of Hawaii Press. They underscore both the solemnity and high excitement with which the news was received on March 12, 1959, that Congress had authorized the admission of Hawaii as the fiftieth state.

On August 21, President Eisenhower signed the proclamation and ordered that the fifty-star flag be made official on July 4, 1960.

Reverend Akaka delivered his sermon in Kawaiahao Church, Honolulu, on March 13, 1959.

"One nation under God, indivisible, with liberty and justice for all"—these words have a fuller meaning for us this morning in Hawaii. And we have gathered here at Kawaiahao Church to give thanks to God, and to pray for His guidance and protection in the years ahead.

[3] Text furnished by the Reverend Abraham K. Akaka, with permission to reprint.

[4] For biographical note, see Appendix.

[5] Reprinted by permission of Thomas Nickerson.

Our newspapers lately have been full of much valuable historical data concerning Hawaii's development, growth, and aspirations. I will keep these stories as long as I live, for my children and their children, for they call to mind the long train of those whose sacrifices were accepted, whose prayers and hopes through the years were fulfilled yesterday. There yet remains the formal expression of our people for statehood, and the entrance of our Islands into the Union as a full-fledged member.

I would like today to speak the message of self-affirmation: that we take courage to be what we truly are, the Aloha State.

On April 25, 1820, one hundred and thirty-nine years ago, the first Christian service conducted in Honolulu was held on this very ground. Like our Pilgrim Fathers who arrived at Plymouth, Massachusetts, in 1620, so did the fathers of a new era in Hawaii kneel in prayer after a long and trying voyage to give thanks to God who had seen them safely on their way.

Gathered around the Reverend Hiram Bingham on that day were a few of our "kupunas" who had come out of curiosity. The text of the sermon that day, though it was April and near Easter time, was from the Christmas Story. And there our people heard these words for the first time:

*Mai maka'u 'oukou, no ka mea, eia ho'i, ke ha'i aku nei au ia 'oukou i ka mea maika'i, e 'oli'oli nui ai e lilo ana no na kanaka apau. No ka mea, i keia la i hanau ai, ma ke kulanakauhale o Davida, he ola no 'oukou, aia ka Mesia ka Haku—*Fear not, for behold, I bring you good tidings of great joy which shall be to all people. For unto you is born this day in the city of David a Saviour which is Christ the Lord.

Although our grandfathers did not realize it fully then, the hopes and fears of all their years through the next century and more were to be met in the meaning and power of those words, for, from that beginning, a new Hawaii was born. For through those words, our missionaries and people following them under God became the greatest single influence in Hawaii's whole development—politically, economically, socially, religiously. Hawaii's real preparation for statehood can be said to have truly begun on that day and on this spot one hundred and thirty-nine years ago.

Yesterday, when the first sound of firecrackers and sirens reached my ears, I was with the members of our Territorial Senate in the middle of the morning prayer for the day's session. How strange it was, and yet how fitting, that the news should burst forth while we were in prayer together. Things had moved so fast. Our mayor, a few minutes before, had asked if the church could be kept open, because he and others wanted to walk across the street for prayer when the news came. By the time I got back from the Senate, this sanctuary was well filled with people who happened to be around, people from our government buildings nearby. And as we sang the great hymns of Hawaii and our nation, it seemed that the very walls of this church spoke of God's dealing with Hawaii in the past, of great events both spontaneous and planned.

There are some of us to whom statehood brings great hopes, and there are some to whom statehood brings silent fears. One might say that the hopes and fears of Hawaii are met in statehood today. There are fears that Hawaii as a state will be motivated by economic greed; that statehood will turn Hawaii (as someone has said) into a great big spiritual junkyard filled with smashed dreams, worn-out illusions; that it will make the Hawaiian people lonely, confused, insecure, empty, anxious, restless, disillusioned—a wistful people.

There is an old *mele* that reminds me of such fears as these, and of the way God leads us out of our fears.

Haku'i i ka uahi o ka lua, pa i ka lani, ha'aha'a Hawai'i moku o Keawe i hanau'ia . . . po Puna, po Hilo, po i ka uahi o ku'u'aina . . . ola ia kini, ke 'a mai la ke ahi—There is a fire underground, but the firepit gives forth only smoke, smoke that bursts upward, touching the skies, and Hawaii is humbled beneath its darkness . . . it is night over Hawaii, night from the smoke of my land . . . but there is salvation for the people, for now the land is being lit by a great flame.

We need to see statehood as the lifting of the clouds of smoke, as the opportunity to affirm positively the basic gospel of the fatherhood of God and the brotherhood of man. We need to see that Hawaii has potential moral and spiritual contributions to make to our nation and to our world. The fears Hawaii may have are to be met by men and women who are living witnesses of what we really are in Hawaii, of the spirit of Aloha, men and women who can help unlock the doors to the future by the guidance and grace of God.

This kind of self-affirmation is the need of the hour. And we can affirm our being, as the Aloha State, by full participation in our nation and in our world. For any collective anxiety, the answer is collective courage. And the ground of that courage is God.

We do not understand the meaning of Aloha until we realize its foundation in the power of God at work in the world. Since the coming of our missionaries in 1820, the name for God to our people has been Aloha. One of the first sentences I learned from my mother in my childhood was this from Holy Scripture: *Aloha ke Akua*—in other words, "God is Aloha." Aloha is the power of God seeking to unite what is separated in the world—the power that unites heart with heart, soul with soul, life with life, culture with culture, race with race, nation with nation. Aloha is the power that can reunite when a quarrel has brought separation; Aloha is the power that reunites a man with himself when he has become separated from the image of God within.

Thus, when a person or a people live in the spirit of Aloha they live in the spirit of God. And among such a people, whose lives so affirm their inner being, we see the working of the Scripture:

All things work together for good to them who love God . . . from the Aloha of God came his Son that we might have life and that we might have it more abundantly.

Aloha consists of this new attitude of heart, above negativism, above legalism. It is the unconditional desire to promote the true good of other people in a friendly spirit, out of a sense of kinship. Aloha seeks to do good, with no conditions attached. We do not do good only to those who do good to us. One of the sweetest things about the love of God, about Aloha, is that it welcomes the stranger and seeks his good. A person who has the spirit of Aloha loves even when the love is not returned. And such is the love of God.

This is the meaning of Aloha. I feel especially grateful that the discovery and development of our Islands long ago was not couched in the context of an imperialistic and exploitive national power, but in this context of Aloha. There is a correlation between the charter under which the missionaries came—namely, "to preach the Gospel of Jesus Christ, to cover these islands with productive green fields, and to lift the people to a high state of civilization"—a correlation between this and the fact that Hawaii is not one of the trouble spots in the world today but one of the spots of great hope. Aloha does not exploit a people or keep them in ignorance and subservience. Rather, it shares the sorrows and joys of people; it seeks to promote the true good of others.

Today, one of the deepest needs of mankind is the need to feel a sense of kinship one with another. Truly all mankind belongs together; from the beginning all mankind has been called into being, nourished, watched over by the love of God. So that the real Golden Rule is Aloha. This is the way of life we shall affirm.

Let us affirm ever what we really are—for Aloha is the spirit of God at work in you and in me and in the world, uniting what is separated, overcoming darkness and death, bringing new light and life to all who sit in the darkness of fear, guiding the feet of mankind into the way of peace.

Thus, may our becoming a state mean to our nation and the world, and may it reaffirm that which was planted in us one hundred and thirty-nine years ago: "Fear not, for behold I bring you good tidings of great joy, which shall be to all people."

PROPOSALS FOR THE ERA OF MIGHT

PEACEFUL CHANGE [1]

CHRISTIAN A. HERTER [2]

The fourteenth session of the General Assembly of the United Nations opened in New York on September 15, 1959. On September 17, Secretary of State Christian A. Herter made his first official address before that body. In an extended report, he presented a virtual summary of the position of the United States on the major problems confronting the community of nations. The United Nations, he declared, had not fully resolved its principal obligation and problem: "that of preventing change through the use of aggressive force, while devising processes to accomplish needed and constructive change through peaceful means." Asserting that the United States accepts the principle of change, he outlined the general pattern of America's hope for disarmament.

Premier Khrushchev appeared the next day before the General Assembly and submitted the Soviet Union's plan for "general and complete disarmament" over a four-year period. October 28 the full membership of the Assembly, in a unique action, sponsored a resolution submitting the substance of Mr. Khrushchev's plan and of the United Kingdom's plan to a ten-nation disarmament conference scheduled to assemble in Geneva in March 1960. On February 18, 1960, before the National Press Club in Washington, D.C., Secretary Herter gave an address entitled "National Security with Arms Limitation." In it he sketched the general features of the disarmament proposal which the Western powers would doubtless submit at the Geneva Conference.

One of Secretary Herter's remarks in the speech before the General Assembly took an ironic turn. He indicated how heartened he was to learn that Soviet jamming of the Voice of America broadcasts had stopped on September 15; and he hoped this change "may prove of long duration." According to George V. Allen, Director of the United States Information Agency, the translation of the Secretary's speech was "jammed heavily."

This, my first appearance before the General Assembly, gives me a welcome opportunity to express my strong belief and firm faith in the United Nations.

[1] Text furnished by Temple Wanamaker, director of the Office of Public Services, Department of State, with permission for this reprint.

[2] For biographical note, see Appendix.

There is a special personal satisfaction to me in being here for this purpose today. A little over forty years ago I served on the staff of a distinguished American President, Woodrow Wilson, when he went to France to negotiate what we then hoped would be an enduring peace. President Wilson held strong convictions concerning the need for an effective international organization to provide means for nations of the world to work together to solve their common problems.

Twenty years ago this month the structure of peace that he had helped to build collapsed in war.

In the backwash of World War II, however, man continued his quest for peace through international organization. The states subscribing to the United Nations Charter at San Francisco in 1945 sought to build a new and more effective instrument for this purpose.

This meeting is one more step in our continuing effort to strengthen that organization and to fulfill its goals.

If all of us devote ourselves faithfully to the task, and thus carry out the obligations of the charter, I believe that we can achieve the peaceful world which people everywhere earnestly desire.

Peaceful Change

To do this, we must deal with a major problem that the League of Nations did not master and that the United Nations has not yet been able fully to resolve: that of preventing change through the use of aggressive force, while devising processes to accomplish needed and constructive change through peaceful means.

The United States accepts the principle of change. Our history, as evidenced by the recent admission of Alaska and Hawaii to the Union, proves the capacity of our system of government to meet and adjust to change.

But the way in which change comes about is of overriding importance in the nuclear age. Attempts to change the international situation through force could destroy us all. Total nuclear war has now become, quite literally, a suicidal enterprise. Peaceful progress, on the other hand, could open up new vistas for all mankind.

The United Nations itself is one of the major instruments both for deterring force and for accomplishing peaceful change.

The United Nations helped to resist force when aggression threatened the Republic of Korea. It helps to deter force through its effort to create standby arrangements, which could enable national contingents to be brought together quickly in meeting any future need for a United Nations force. We hope that members will respond positively to the Secretary-General's efforts in this regard.

The United Nations assists peaceful change through fact-finding and conciliation processes, which can help to prevent disputes from exploding into wider conflict.

The United States stands ready to work peacefully, within the framework of the charter, with all states which share our objectives of insuring peaceful progress.

The Past Year

The past year has seen continued movement toward this goal of peaceful change, on the one hand, and renewed threats of violence which would impede its fulfillment, on the other.

Progress has been encouraging, in comparison with the situation existing at this time a year ago, in five major areas.

In the Middle East a period of relative quiet prevails. This is in sharp contrast to the crisis of a year ago, when the Assembly had to take important emergency measures. The enlightened actions of the states in the area during the past year have helped to improve the situation. The agencies of the United Nations and the outstanding leadership and diplomacy of the Secretary-General have also contributed significantly to the lessening of tensions and the development of greater stability.

We regard these trends as a hopeful portent that further progress can be made on the problems which still confront this area.

The future welfare of the Palestine refugees is one such problem. It will be an important item for consideration at this

Assembly. Progress toward a satisfactory solution of this tragic problem is important not only to the human beings directly involved but also to continued peace and stability in the area as a whole.

Another problem in this area has arisen with regard to passage through the Suez Canal. The United States continues to support the principle of freedom of passage, as endorsed by the United Nations. We are confident that, if those immediately concerned seek to reconcile their differences in a spirit of mutual accommodation, progress can be made toward a solution.

Africa is an area where there has also been steady forward movement. Four new African states are to achieve independence in the coming year. Progress toward self-government is a development which the United States welcomes, in accordance with its historic policy that all peoples should have independence who desire it and are able to undertake its responsibilities.

Political advancement in the non-self-governing and trust territories of Africa is a tribute to the imagination, good will, and skill of the peoples of those territories and of the powers that administer them. It is also a tribute to the encouragement and assistance given by the United Nations and the specialized agencies to the advancement of these territories.

In Europe the North Atlantic Treaty Organization has continued to grow in peaceful power during the last year. It now represents an even more formidable bulwark of peace in support of the principles of the charter. President Eisenhower's recent visit to the NATO area has produced new evidence of the unity, strength, and purpose of the Atlantic Community.

We welcome particularly the progress that has been made during the past year toward a just solution of the Cyprus problem, which directly concerns three of the NATO countries. These countries and the people of Cyprus are to be congratulated on this progress.

In Latin America important steps have been taken in the last year to strengthen the peace machinery of the Organization of American States. The recent conference of the foreign ministers of the American republics in Santiago is an encouraging example of how a regional organization can complement the work of the

United Nations. It clearly demonstrated the determination of the American republics to maintain peace in the hemisphere through common action on problems creating international tensions.

The Far East has also seen continued progress during the past year in promoting domestic welfare and in strengthening security. War-torn economies have been, for the most part, rebuilt and the foundations laid for further progress.

We regret that the republics of Korea and Vietnam are still excluded by the veto of one power from United Nations membership, although both have been found fully qualified by the General Assembly.

The member countries of the Southeast Asia Treaty Organization have carried forward their programs for economic, social, and cultural advancement. SEATO also plays a vital role in the collective defense of the area and is now carefully watching events in Laos.

Side by side with these encouraging developments, which augur well for peaceful and constructive change, events in the past year have underlined the continuing danger posed by attempts to mold the international situation through the threat or use of force.

Most recently the freedom and independence of Laos have been threatened by forces from outside its borders. The Security Council subcommittee is now in Laos. We hope that it will not only succeed in collecting the facts but also by its presence contribute to easing a potentially dangerous situation.

In this circumstance there is no need for a conference as proposed by the USSR. Such a conference would be disruptive and would ignore the authority of the United Nations.

This recent action of the Security Council demonstrates the ability of the United Nations to act quickly in a case involving possible efforts to subvert the freedom and undermine the security of member states.

The United States is pledged under the charter to resist aggression. It will fulfill this pledge without equivocation. We will support the royal Laos Government in its own efforts to preserve independence.

In Tibet we are confronted by the revolting spectacle of the brutal Chinese Communist repression of the fundamental human rights of the Tibetans. The Dalai Lama under threat of force was driven from his country. From his exile in India, he has told the world a tragic story of persecution, of forced labor, of deportation, of executions in such numbers as to threaten the survival of the Tibetan race. Yet the Tibetans' only crime was their desire to live in peace and freedom. This is a matter which is of deep concern to the United Nations. Certainly this organization must speak out in clear terms in the face of such events.

In the Taiwan Strait area, where last year at this time we were seriously concerned by the military action of the Chinese Communists, Communist China has continued its sporadic campaign of military harassment. Despite months of negotiations it refuses to renounce the use of force.

In Korea the Chinese Communist regime continues to reject the principles for unification that would assure the freedom and independence of a united Korea. It has flouted the terms of the armistice in Korea. It still stands condemned as an aggressor.

In supporting efforts to subvert the will of the free people of Laos, in attempting to exterminate the people of Tibet, and in its incursions into India, the Chinese Communist regime has demonstrated more clearly in the past year than at any time since its aggression in Korea its complete unfitness to be admitted to this organization. We are confident that the members of this Assembly will continue to resist efforts to obtain China's seat in the United Nations for the Communist regime.

That seat is honorably occupied by the representative of the republic of China, a charter member of this organization. That republic has given renewed evidence of its continuing dedication to the principles of this organization in the past year by its historic declaration that it would rely primarily upon peaceful principles and not upon force to secure the freeing of the mainland.

Hungary is another area where the effects of the threat and use of violence are manifest. The tyrannical rule which was imposed on that unhappy country by the ruthless use of outside force still obtains. Every effort of Sir Leslie Munro, the Assembly's special representative, to investigate the situation first-hand has been rebuffed by the puppet Hungarian regime, which Soviet troops imposed and now maintain. The continued, deliberate defiance by Hungary of this organization augurs ill for our continuing efforts to secure international peace and security.

These events of the past year must be viewed in perspective. The progress that has been achieved testifies to the opportunities which lie ahead. Continuing threats of force and violence underline the dangers which still confront us.

To avert these dangers and fulfill those opportunities, we must seek to promote peaceful change which will lay the basis for a just and lasting peace. We must seek such change in political, military, economic, and other fields.

Political Change: Germany and Berlin

We will always negotiate with other states to achieve peaceful political change which derives from the freely given consent of the peoples concerned. Our approach to the Geneva negotiations on Germany and Berlin reflected this philosophy in concrete terms.

I spent ten long weeks in Geneva with the Foreign Ministers of France, the United Kingdom, and the USSR in seeking agreement on the problem of a divided Germany and a divided Berlin.

The Geneva conference met against the backdrop of a potential crisis over Berlin. This had been artificially precipitated by a Soviet threat to take unilateral action against West Berlin. It was only after this threat had been withdrawn that the Western powers agreed to negotiate in the interests of peaceful change.

The governments of France, the United Kingdom, and the United States had as their purpose at Geneva to secure the reunification of Germany in freedom. Such peaceful change would have solved the Berlin question on a lasting basis by restoring Berlin to its rightful place as the capital of a united Germany.

To this end the Western powers put forward a comprehensive Western peace plan. That plan was designed to achieve the reunification of Germany according to the will of the German people and on a basis which took into account the expressed concerns of the Soviet Union.

The Western peace plan was a phased plan which provided time for a mixed German committee to draft an electoral law and to work out proposals for increased technical contacts between the two parts of Germany and for freedom of movement and respect for human rights throughout all of Germany. While this process went on, there would be related preliminary steps for the exchange of military information, for the limitation of over-all strength of the forces of the four powers, and for measures of inspection against surprise attack.

In the next phase safeguarded elections for an all-German assembly would be held. This all-German assembly would draft a constitution on the basis of which an all-German government would be formed. That government would then be responsible for negotiating an all-German peace treaty.

In this phase further disarmament and security measures were contemplated, including the establishment of a zone on either side of a line to be mutually determined in which there would be agreed ceilings for the indigenous and nonindigenous forces.

Moreover, if the all-German government decided to adhere either to NATO or the Warsaw Pact, additional security arrangements were to be made. These would contemplate special measures regulating the disposition of forces in the area closest to the eastern frontier of a united Germany. They would provide for agreements between the four powers and other European countries about joint reaction against aggression.

Unhappily—and I use the word advisedly—the Soviet Foreign Minister Andrei A. Gromyko rejected the Western peace plan out of hand. He seemed disinterested in studying this carefully devised program, to which the Western governments had devoted many months of preparation.

The conference then turned to the question of how to arrive at a *modus vivendi* on Berlin which would ease the tensions that the Soviet Union itself had created.

For this purpose the Western powers made many proposals. All of them seemed to meet aspects of the problem concerning which the Soviets complained. None jeopardized the freedom and the security of the people of West Berlin.

What we must never forget is that the problem of West Berlin is not really a legal problem or an abstract case history in political science. It is the matter of the lives and freedom and happiness of these more than two million people who live in West Berlin, people who have shown by their courage and the fruits of their labor the blessings that freedom brings.

These people are surrounded by territory and forces under the control of an unfriendly regime. They rely on the presence of the token contingents of American, British, and French troops for their security.

The long-drawn-out discussion of this problem of Berlin resulted in no agreement. The negotiations did, however, usefully isolate the areas of possible agreement. That is why the foreign ministers of France, the United Kingdom, and the United States have some hope that a resumed foreign ministers conference can agree on arrangements for Berlin which would safeguard the future of the West Berliners.

Through their dedication to this continuing negotiation, the Western powers evidence their support for the process of peaceful change in the political field.

Military Change: Arms Limitation and Control

Acceptance of this process would be of at least equal importance in the military field.

Perhaps the greatest contribution that could be made to peaceful change would be for the powers to move from reliance on unlimited arms competition to reliance on safeguarded agreements as a means of preserving national security.

During the past year there have been both promising and disappointing developments with respect to our efforts in this field, which are of such critical importance to the future of all mankind.

The United States took the initiative in proposing a technical conference on measures to guard against surprise attack. While the problems are understood more clearly as a result, we regret that little progress was made.

The United States and United Kingdom continued the negotiations begun a year ago with the USSR for an agreement on the discontinuance of nuclear weapons testing. There is some progress to report. The three powers have agreed on a number of details which would have to be a part of a full accord, and technical agreement has been recently reached on the means of detecting and identifying nuclear explosives at high altitudes and in outer space.

However, there are still three central issues on which agreement has not been achieved. They all relate to effective inspection, which remains the key to agreement.

First, there is the problem of staffing control posts—"the listening posts" that would be established to register data which might indicate an unauthorized nuclear explosion.

The Soviet Union has insisted that a major portion of the personnel at each control post must be from the host country, a form of "self-inspection" which we cannot accept.

The United States and the United Kingdom have proposed that all technical and supervisory positions at each post be staffed on the basis of one third U.S. or U.K. specialists, one third Soviet specialists, and one third specialists from countries other than these three. This would allow for reasonable host-country representation. It would be a genuinely international staffing pattern in which all countries could have confidence. Finally, it would provide a role for other members of the United Nations, who have a deep interest in assuring a successfully operating system.

The second key control issue is the matter of on-site inspections required to identify suspected underground explosions.

While the United States does not object to placing a limit on these inspections, we believe that the number should be based on a scientific judgment, not on political arguments.

To assist in making this judgment we have submitted scientific data bearing on the complex problem of detecting underground explosions and determining whether they are nuclear explosions or earthquakes. We remain convinced that this information should be considered, although the Soviet Union has thus far refused to do so.

The third key issue in the negotiations is the veto.

The Soviet Union wants the veto in one form or another. The United States firmly believes that any control system which could be frustrated in its day-to-day operations by the veto power would be worse than useless. It would create the illusion and not the reality of control.

These are the principal issues. It is clear that the points at issue are real. They cannot be ignored.

We hope that these three issues can be resolved and that an agreement can be achieved for a comprehensive test ban. We will pursue this approach with vigor, but there *is* another approach if the Soviets are not willing to agree to the necessary means of verification.

On April 13 of this year President Eisenhower offered to Chairman Khrushchev to enter immediately into an agreement to ban tests within the atmosphere and under water, if the Soviet Union remained unwilling to accept effective safeguards for a complete discontinuance of nuclear weapons tests.

This would be only a first step toward the ultimate objective of a total ban. However, it would represent a very good start. It would also ease concern over levels of radioactivity. This offer still stands.

In the meantime, President Eisenhower recently announced that the one-year unilateral ban on tests which the United States voluntarily undertook last October would be continued to the end of this year. Our hope is that, if we allow a reasonable extension of time for the negotiations to proceed, significant progress can be made.

These are the principal developments regarding a possible agreement on a comprehensive test ban.

But the question of disarmament is much broader than suspension of nuclear testing. What we earnestly seek is the general limitation and control of armaments and armed forces. The degree to which we succeed may determine man's future. There would be growing danger in an indefinite continuation of the arms race. We must use all of our imagination and ingenuity to devise a way of controlling this race, to prevent it from exploding into nuclear conflict.

In an effort to renew disarmament negotiations, the United States and the United Kingdom and France have agreed with the Soviet Union, with which they share a major responsibility for reaching a solution on this problem, to resume discussions on disarmament early next year. These four powers have invited a small group of other states to join them.

The United States regards the coming negotiations as a major opportunity. We hope that the Soviet Government will view them with equal seriousness. Successful negotiations could not only open new avenues of progress toward limitation and control of armaments but also pave the way for settlement of other outstanding problems.

Peaceful Uses of Outer Space

Recognizing that progress in disarmament might be slow, however, the United States has urged that peaceful uses of outer space be considered as a separate step toward constructive change.

Last year my distinguished predecessor, John Foster Dulles, proposed that the General Assembly take the first step toward establishing a framework for international cooperation in this field. The United States hoped then that it would prove possible for all members to share in the benefits that seem certain to emerge from this challenging new frontier of human activity.

Recent events have demonstrated how rapidly this frontier is being crossed. The American "paddlewheel," Explorer VI, still circles the earth six weeks after its launching, sending messages back to earth with energy from the sun. We believe this development advances the day when nations of the world will be linked by a communications network extending to the heavens.

The Soviet moon probe—certainly a great accomplishment—foreshadows the early extension of terrestrial problems out into the universe. It also warns us to speed up our efforts to obtain peace on earth. And it signals the pressing need to get on with international arrangements to make a start on the regulation of man's activities away from his earthly home.

In the early years after the development of atomic energy the United States tried long and hard to interest the USSR in an international approach to harnessing this natural force of such great danger and promise to humanity. The USSR refused to cooperate, apparently believing that its late start in the atomic energy field would prejudice its national interests if an international approach were adopted. The deadly arms race of the past decade stands as an ugly witness to the human tragedy of that Soviet noncooperation.

Now humanity is on the threshold of another and perhaps more fateful technological development—the penetration of outer space. Again the United States has called for an international approach. This time surely the USSR cannot plead a lack of Soviet advancement in this technology. But we see little sign of any Soviet disposition to cooperate as yet. The Soviets have declined to participate in the work of the United Nations committee this past year.

Arguing that only the USSR and the United States were carrying on activities in the field of outer space, the Soviet Union contended that the Committee should be made up of an equal number of states from these "two sides." This concept was rejected by the Assembly. The world is not divided into two "hostile camps," as the Soviet Union maintains. The world is diverse. This concept is inherent in the United Nations.

The United States believes that major committees of the United Nations should continue to reflect the principle of fair geographical representation. This principle derogates in no way from the relative contribution which those states with superior technical capacity can make.

We hope that the Soviet Union will join in the cooperative efforts of the United Nations. There could be no more dramatic illustration of a spirit of cooperation in the world today as we stand at the threshold of the space age than for this Assembly to act unanimously in this field. This would be a major step forward in the process of peaceful change.

Economic and Social Change

Peaceful change in the economic and social field is also of key importance if our purposes are to be fulfilled.

The United Nations is contributing to social progress through its activities in such fields as health, refugee assistance, narcotics, and the Children's Fund.

Economic improvement can be promoted by healthy competitive trade, which helps assure greater enjoyment of the fruits of economic activity, and by continuing economic development.

Last year Mr. Dulles proposed that the nations dedicate the year 1959 to taking stock of their current accomplishments in the field of economic development and to charting long-term courses of action. The United States has now taken the major steps which Secretary Dulles said that we would take in this field.

First, the United States has vigorously pressed its development financing programs. The Congress has appropriated additional funds for the Development Loan Fund. The flexibility possible in the administration of this Fund enhances its importance as a source of loans for less-developed countries.

Second, the United States and other nations have doubled their subscriptions to the International Bank for Reconstruction and Development and have increased their subscriptions to the International Monetary Fund by 50 per cent in the past year.

Third, the United States will propose to the forthcoming meeting of the governors of the International Bank a resolution calling for definite steps toward the prompt establishment of an international development association. Such an organization will provide a new and effective means of financing in less developed countries sound high priority projects which cannot be adequately aided under existing criteria of the International Bank.

Fourth, United States acceptance of the agreement for the establishment of the Inter-American Development Bank has been approved by our Congress. Establishment of this institution will help to hasten the development of the countries of the Western Hemisphere.

Fifth, the United States continues and will continue, in co-operation with other member states, to give full support to existing organizations devoted to the extension of technical assistance. We are gratified that the newly established special fund has taken hold so quickly and begun its important opera-tions. It is my strong hope that other member governments will find it possible to increase their contribution to both the ex-panded program and the special fund in order that the initial goal of $100 million for both programs can be reached as soon as possible.

In these and other ways the United States dedicates its re-sources and energies to the only kind of world war that any of us can hope to win: war on poverty, on disease, and on illiteracy.

The fact that more than a billion and a half people of this world live in dire want poses a challenge to which we must respond. To try to escape this challenge would deny the com-mon bond that joins all human beings regardless of race, sex, language, or religion.

Make no mistake about it: Wherever men despair of being able to meet their needs through peaceful means, there will be found the seeds of tyranny and conflict. If peaceful change is to be accomplished in the political and military field, it must also go forward at an increasing pace in the economic field.

The Need for "Open Societies"

There is one other avenue to peace and peaceful change which I would like to mention before I close, Mr. President. This avenue is to achieve that "world community of open societies" which President Eisenhower stressed at the 1958 emergency session. This "openness" has long been a fundamental characteristic of American society and of many other free societies. The achievement of "open societies" could make an important contribution to peace.

But it must be recognized that this goal cannot be fully achieved as long as governments and regimes disregard the basic principles of international conduct. Realizing this, we regret the need for maintaining safeguards in the interest of peace and stability. For example, the concept of "open societies" cannot be fully achieved as long as the Chinese Communist regime uses increased contacts to subvert and to undermine neighboring peoples and countries.

Within a number of other countries artificial barriers still exist to free, open, and friendly communications.

There are barriers of secrecy and of artificial restrictions.

There is censorship of the printed and broadcast word.

There is jamming of radio broadcasts from without, jamming based on fear that uncensored information may incidentally enter. Let me say right here, however, how heartened we have been to note that Soviet jamming of the Voice of America ceased on September 15. We profoundly hope that this beneficial change may prove of long duration.

There are rules which severely limit contact of nationals with foreign visitors or travel from one part of the country to another.

Behind such barriers are bred images, false reports, and false fears of imaginary enemies. These conditions feed upon themselves. They contribute to needless arming and counterarming. They can give a powerful impetus to the spiral that leads toward war. So long as such barriers exist to the flow of news and information into a country, we cannot even begin to weave the fabric of lasting peace.

Openness is particularly important in those countries possessing great destructive power and which bear a great responsibility for peace.

Today, when we take stock of the situation, two impressions stand out.

First, encouraging beginnings in breaking through these barriers have been made.

Second, there are additional areas in which further removal of restrictions would be helpful to the cause of peace.

Recent developments within the Soviet Union, despite their limited scope, provide a glimmer of hope that the Soviet Government may be willing to permit a freer exchange of ideas and information between its own people and other peoples. These developments permit the hope that the Soviet Government may now be prepared to go even further. They prompt me to make a proposal comparable to the one the United States put forward during a Security Council session last year—that the Soviet radio transmitters suspend their jamming sufficiently to permit the Soviet people to hear in full the proceedings of the fourteenth session of the General Assembly now beginning.

The debates in the Assembly are extremely useful in indicating the numerous and diverse viewpoints which are held on a variety of international issues. Public knowledge of these viewpoints cannot be regarded as subversive to any government regardless of its structure or policies.

Conclusion

We have thus sought and continue to seek peaceful change through many approaches.

These efforts draw force and inspiration from the work of the United Nations. Under its charter the United Nations is pledged to resist aggressive force. It can be the real catalyst in the process of constructive change.

In assisting this process all members of the United Nations, large and small, have a voice. Bringing diverse viewpoints to bear while respecting each other's interests and viewpoints, the members of the United Nations are united in a common effort, in the words of the preamble of the charter, "to save succeeding generations from the scourge of war, which twice in our lifetime has brought untold sorrow to mankind" and "to promote social progress and better standards of life in larger freedom."

The principles of the charter directly reflect the precepts of all the great religions. Let us then proceed to the task of fulfilling these principles. In the words of Abraham Lincoln, ". . . with firmness in the right as God gives us to see the right, let us strive on to finish the work we are in . . . to do all which may achieve and cherish a just and lasting peace. . . ."

The United States here rededicates itself to this noble effort to achieve peace and justice for all mankind.

THE DISMANTLING OF THE ERA OF TERROR[3]

Thomas E. Murray [4]

Disarmament and the control of atomic weapons constitute the most serious concern of mankind. Ever since the first atomic bombs were dropped in 1945, proposals for controlling the production and use of such weapons have been continually under consideration. The most recent effort to bring about a ban on nuclear tests is the Geneva Conference at which representatives from the Soviet Union, Great Britain, and the United States have conferred since 1958. During this period the United States held to its temporary moratorium on atomic tests.

On December 9, 1959, in a speech before the Institute of World Affairs at Pasadena, California, Thomas E. Murray, former commissioner of the Atomic Energy Commission, set forth a striking proposal for disarmament. In a subsequent report to the Chairman of the Joint Committee on Atomic Energy, he elaborated upon the implications of his plan and upon his reasons for believing that "potentially grave security dangers" lurk within the current disarmament policy of the United States. "The main reason behind my proposal," he reported, "is the urgent need to design a practical alternative policy which will permit the U.S. to seize the initiative in the field of disarmament without impairing national security."

On August 29, 1949, when the Soviet Union exploded its first atomic device, a new era began in the long history of the relations between politics and force. During the ensuing decade the pace of political and technological change has been so swift that men are now beginning to say that we have reached the end of the era that began in 1949.

One general judgment of the era is becoming increasingly common. We now realize that the immense drive to arm the United States with nuclear weapons and delivery systems has not been guided and controlled by a clear and practical national purpose. In particular, five criticisms are gaining currency.

First, our armament effort has been wrongly subject to the domination of technology. We have failed to submit tech-

[3] Text furnished by Thomas E. Murray, with permission for this reprint.
[4] For biographical note, see Appendix.

nological possibilities to the criterion of military and political usefulness. Second, the result has been an emphasis on the strategy of unlimited war, as exhibited in the concept of massive retaliation. Third, the further result has been a complete divorce between military strategy and political aims. Our dominant military strategy and its supporting arms look to the release of unlimited power, whereas our political aims, whatever they may be, are certainly not unlimited. Fourth, and again in consequence, in the very midst of the enormous power-struggle now going on in the world arena, our foreign policies lack the necessary support of force. Our military "strength" has degenerated into a mere capacity to wreak unlimited nuclear violence, which is politically useless; and this very capacity inhibits us from the use of limited force, which may be politically necessary. Fifth, this whole disorderly structure of policy stands under the final peril, which is a lack of moral sanction. It is against the dictates of reason that military strategy should accept the control of technology. Politics, not technology, is the rightful master of military doctrine. It is also against the dictates of reason that the use of force, which may be the necessary instrument of justice, should suffer moral degradation and become a sheer exercise in violence, which can serve no moral or political purposes.

These five criticisms are entirely valid. If I may say so, I had made them myself before their validity began to be commonly recognized. Taken together, they demonstrate the instant need for a new design of American policy, guided by a new vision of the public purpose of America.

The danger of the moment is that American disarmament policies during the decade to come will be characterized by the same confusions that have marked our armament policies in the decade that is past. We swung into action on armament without stopping to put right order in our thought. We have already swung into action on disarmament without stopping to correct the disorders of thought that have already proved so pernicious and will prove pernicious again.

The first problem then is to define the public purpose of America in the field of disarmament. The basis of definition must be the essential distinction between violence and force. This is a political distinction, based on a moral premise. By violence I mean the use of military power in such an extensive, indiscriminating, or even unlimited, measure and manner that its use becomes inept and useless for the rational purposes of politics, which are always limited. By force I mean the use of power in such a limited measure and in such a discriminating manner that its use becomes an apt instrument for the achievement of legitimate political goals. The release of violence is irrational and therefore immoral but the use of force, as thus defined can be rightful, depending on the political rationality and moral rightness of the particular purposes for which it is used.

The past decade has been an Era of Terror because over it has hung the threat of violence—uncontrolled, unlimited, both politically and morally absurd. Our immediate and urgent purpose, therefore, must be to effect an orderly dismantling of the Era of Terror, by dissipating this threat of violence. This negative purpose must be allied with the more positive purpose of effecting the orderly construction of a new era. One cannot give it a name or fully describe it. But its essential characteristic must be the reinstatement of force as an instrument for the basic political purpose that is indicated in the American Constitution, namely, "to establish justice."

Given the nature of man, the art of international politics cannot dispense with the use, or at least the threat, of force, any more than human society can dispense with law, which requires force to back it up. On the other hand, international politics perishes as an art if power is allowed to suffer moral degradation and become mere violence, which is destructive of the very idea of force and of law too.

This statement of the two-fold national purpose of America immediately serves to make it clear that nuclear tests are not the primary or most important issue. The past decade has not been the Era of Terror because it has been an era of tests. The current moratorium on all tests has done nothing to banish the threat of violence. This threat derives from the escape of nuclear technology from the control of military doctrine and political purpose. Here the primary issue appears. Technology does not know the difference between violence and force. Left to itself, without the control of higher policy, it has tended to enlarge our capacity to wreak violence, not to use force. Government, however, is supposed to know this essential political and moral distinction. And it is the duty of government, by political decision, to make the implications of the distinction binding both on the deliberations of the military strategist and on the experiments of the technological expert.

The primary issue therefore is a reform of thought, to be expressed in political decisions. Moreover, it is not difficult to discern the direction that political decision must take, if it is to rectify its own past errors and retrieve its own past failures. The disorders of policy in the past decade have left as their fateful legacy a great and ever growing stockpile of weapons of violence —megaton weapons whose destructive capacity is unlimited, if used in the numbers required by the current strategy of massive retaliation. We must assume that the Soviet stockpile matches our own. The sheer existence of these stockpiles is the proximate reason why the past decade has been an Era of Terror. These stockpiles have created their own strategy, which is that of war of annihilation. And the threat of annihilation has in turn created the terror.

It follows in all logic that the Era of Terror will not be dismantled until these megaton stockpiles are themselves dismantled. This is the immediate issue presented for political decision. The decision does not fall to the strategist or to the technologist. It falls squarely within the province of politics; for it is an issue that concerns the public purpose of the United States. The making of this decision by government is the very condition for the restoration of politics to its rightful place of primacy in the structure of American policy. There is no other way in which the present rupture between political purpose and military strategy can be healed in its depths.

I should like, first, to present in general outline the form that this political decision should take, and then construct the argument, pro and con.

My suggestion has two parts. First, that an international agency be constituted and located on neutral territory and empowered to supervise the systematic destruction of the megaton weapons in the American and Soviet stockpiles. Second, that the destruction be done on a matching basis, weapon for equal weapon. The United States will hand over to the international agency one megaton weapon, beginning in the highest range; the Soviet Union will in turn hand over one weapon of the same size. Experts in the agency will be able to estimate, within a small percentage of error, whether the weapons are equal in their yield. The "hardware" of the weapons will then be destroyed in some public fashion. Their content of highly enriched fissionable material will be put at the disposal of the appropriate international authority for peaceful uses. This matching of weapons, one for one, will continue. The process has a political purpose—to end the Era of Terror, to banish the threat of violence, to redeem force from its moral degradation and its political absurdity. The process will therefore continue until this political purpose, under "a decent respect to the opinions of mankind," has been achieved.

Considerable detail ought to be added to this proposal; but the presentation of its substance is sufficient for the purposes of immediate public debate. I shall undertake to make the case for it.

In the first place, this proposal takes far more realistic account of the needs of national security than does current American disarmament policy. Our present policy was announced at the London conference of 1956, and it has not been changed. It calls for nuclear disarmament: first, by the cessation of all nuclear tests; second, by the stoppage of the flow of fissionable material into weapons; third, by the total destruction of all existing nuclear stockpiles. This proposal clearly illustrates our fatal habit of divorcing political and military policies. For political reasons we declared a moratorium on all tests, despite the fact that military reasons demanded certain kinds of tests. These tests would develop what I have called the third generation of weapons. They would be carried out underground and give us new types of much needed limited weapons, defensive and offensive, which could be used in discriminating fashion. Moreover, the other parts of the proposal, if carried out, would be fatal to any rational concept of American military strength. The program would strip us, not only of the capacity for unlimited and useless nuclear violence, but also of the most useful and necessary capacity to use limited nuclear force.

It is true that the carrying out of the present program was made contingent on the establishment of international inspection and controls. However, in the matter of tests it is clear to informed people that an adequate and effective inspection system, which would detect tests even down to five or ten kilotons, is for the present not a definite scientific possibility, and it is also, for the foreseeable future, a political impossibility. An adequate and effective system would have to consist of thousands of stations, equipped with devices not yet invented; this is the scientific problem. Many hundreds of these stations would have to be on Soviet and Red Chinese territory; this is the political impossibility.

Moreover, the stoppage of all nuclear production and the total destruction of existing stockpiles—stand even farther beyond the possibility of control for scientific and political reasons. Therefore, the first argument for my new proposal lies in the need to find a safe alternative to the extremely risky and altogether unrealistic policy to which we are presently committed.

In the second place, the new proposal goes to the heart of the issue. It is the sinister stockpiles of megaton weapons, and the strategies of annihilation built on them, which give off the fumes of terror that today are poisoning the international atmosphere. The terror has to be attacked at its source, which is the bilateral and balancing power of the United States and the Soviet Union to wreck the fabric of civilization in a matter of hours. These pools of potentially unlimited violence must be drained and dried. All other issues are secondary to this.

In the third place, this proposal is practical. It should be possible to negotiate an agreement on it between ourselves and the Soviet Union, the only two necessary partners to such an agreement. The single indispensable condition of agreement exists, namely, self-interest, hard and cold self-interest, the common and coincident self-interest of both parties. It is as much in the interests of the Soviet Union as it is in our own to avoid the ultimate catastrophe in which the Era of Terror may culminate, if it is not deliberately brought to an end. No national interest, American or Russian, is served by maintaining and increasing a stockpile of weapons of violence that are utterly useless for any political purpose, Russian or American. The political absurdity of unlimited nuclear violence—reciprocally acknowledged—this is the basic fact on which, as on solid ground, an agreement can be based. In the course of their rivalry for megaton armament the U.S. and the USSR have both been driven into an absurd situation. There is a common interest in putting an end to it.

Moreover, the proposal is practical for another reason. It avoids the political stone wall into which other American proposals have always run. This stone wall is set up by the Soviet concept of absolute national sovereignty which forbids honest and effective international inspection of Soviet territory. A new formula has to be found to establish the principle of international control. The proposal I am discussing contains this new formula. It does not call for inspection of Soviet territory.

In the fourth place, this new proposal will inevitably find favor in the court of world opinion. This is what the nations really want—that the United States should take the lead in bringing them out from under the shadow of possible annihilation. The Soviet Union could not refuse to follow this lead without incurring the political punishment of the disfavor of the nations. Moreover, by making this proposal the United States would finally assume the initiative in the problem of disarmament. In all negotiations the party that defines the issue has already gained the initiative. We lost it by giving way under pressure and allowing the Soviet Union to define, as the primary issue in disarmament, the cessation of all tests. This was a grave mistake on many counts. We shall rectify it, and gather the initiative into our own hands, only if we ourselves define the real issue that rightfully claims primacy. This primary issue is the stockpiled capacity for unlimited violence.

In the fifth place, if megaton means of wreaking violence were thus gradually to be destroyed by mutual agreement, the threat of violence would cease to be of use as an instrument of international politics. It would be absurd for a nation to begin surrendering its weapons of terror, and at the same time go on brandishing the threat of their use. Nuclear blackmail would be at an end. The international atmosphere would be considerably cleared.

In the sixth place, the essential distinction between the cold war and the Era of Terror would begin to be realized. The cold war had begun before the Era of Terror set in; it will continue after the terror is ended. Basically, the cold war is a crisis in civilization. The contest is between opposed conceptions of the nature of man, his role in history, and his relation to the state. This ideological conflict has carried over into the field of politics; and its economic dimension is continually growing. During the Era of Terror it has also acquired a military dimension of altogether swollen proportions. Until this military dimension is cut down to proper size, the real issues in the cold war will be obscured.

In particular, it is absolutely necessary to remove from the cold war the issue of sheer physical survival. This issue has done nothing but darken counsel, paralyze purpose, and confuse policy. The issue is fundamentally false; survival should never be an issue in political struggles or even in war. But a nightmarish sort of reality attaches to the issue of survival because of the megaton stockpiles whose use would imperil the survival of everybody. Until these weapons are destroyed, the issue of survival will continue to distract the mind of America from its real job. The public purpose of America in opposing world communism will remain blurred, undefined to ourselves, to the Soviet Union, and to all the world.

In the seventh place, a most salutary effect would be produced on American strategic thought. At least since 1953 it has stood under the hypnotic influence of megaton technology. Its focus has been fixed on the strategy of annihilation. The concept of massive retaliation has held it in deadly thrall. The spell can only be broken by the political decision to enforce the primacy of politics and to begin an orderly surrender of weapons that are politically useless. This decision would compel the military strategist to take new thought. There could at last take place a movement towards increased flexibility in strategic thinking, towards a revival of the traditional principle that the aim of a general is the will of the opposing commander, not the butchery of his forces, still less the total destruction of his country and the indiscriminate slaughter of its civilian population. Thus military doctrine would find its way to rightful relation with political aims. The fatal rupture would come to an end. And with this change in strategy from emphasis on inept violence to emphasis on apt force the technology of weapons would at last be brought under proper rule and restraint. The tail of technology would cease to fly the kite of strategy.

In the eighth place, a step would be taken toward the positive goal of American disarmament policy. The distant goal, still far over the horizon of the future, is the gradual transfer of the right to use arms and to produce nuclear arms, to some new kind of international authority. A small step toward this goal would be taken by establishing an international agency empowered to supervise the destruction of weapons of violence. This assignment is very limited. But the new agency would embody the essential principle of international control of nuclear armament. The principle would have been publicly recognized in the face of the nations and extensions of it would gradually become possible.

In the ninth place, a considerable amount of highly enriched fissionable material would become available, presumably to the International Atomic Energy Agency, for peaceful purposes particularly for the development of industrial nuclear power. This fact would give a tremendous and badly needed impulse to the whole program of Atoms for Peace. This development would have important consequences both in the improvement of international relations as well as in the advance of economic progress.

Here then are the reasons in favor of the proposal. What are the reasons against it? There are only two.

First, it will be said that an agreement to match the Soviet Union in the destruction of weapons of violence would impair the military strength of the U.S.

This objection rests on a false concept of strength. I do not consider it strength on our part to consent to the current degradation of force into violence. On the contrary, it is weakness. Surely, it is moral weakness. It is a failure of the moral intelligence to understand what is going on, or a want of moral courage to stop this process of corruption. It is also political weakness. It is a failure of the political intelligence to see the absurdity of violence, and to see also the rational necessity of force, for the purposes of politics. Moreover, unless this process of moral degradation is checked by the courage of political decision, the result will be to continue and increase our military weakness, the weakness of a nuclear establishment whose political uselessness grows more and more apparent, and the weakness of a technology, whose resources of power are exploited without purpose, because they lack due military and political direction.

It is becoming apparent today that we have been pursuing an illusion of strength along a dead-end road, the same dead-end road into which technology turned military doctrine in 1953, when the hydrogen bomb assumed control of strategy. Since that day our nuclear superiority has been lost. A balance of nuclear power has been established. In this new situation the strategy of ultimate deterrence plus massive retaliation and the megaton stockpile which supports this strategy have lost whatever value, both military and political, they may once have had in the past day of our nuclear superiority.

The conclusion is that we ought now to make some political use of this stockpile since it has been a military liability. Self-interest presently dictates that we trade in our great weapons of violence, one for one, with the Soviet Union doing the same, as a political deal with a political purpose. This act of self-interest would also be an act of the moral conscience of America and a declaration of our civilized public purpose. We would give witness in action that we shall not abdicate the right uses of force, but that we do abjure the senseless uses of violence, because we understand that politics needs force, but morals condemn violence.

The second objection raises the ultimate question: Would the proposed action invite massive Soviet aggression and open the U.S. to defeat and destruction? Would not the Soviet Union "cheat on" the agreement in order to gain nuclear superiority in megaton weapons, and then would it not, at some given moment, launch a total attack on the U.S.?

This possibility cannot be absolutely excluded. Here is the irreducible risk. No policy can take account of every single future possibility. Policy directs itself to what is likely to happen, not to what may possibly happen. Risks must always be calculated. On any fair calculation the risk involved in my proposal is minimal. Certainly it is far less serious than the risk involved in the present American disarmament proposal.

It has to be remembered that the distinction between force and violence, which I am urging as the basic premise of American policy, does in fact constitute the basic premise of Soviet policy. In contrast communism is not committed to the political ineptitude of unlimited violence. The Communist purpose is always to use apt force, whenever it is useful or necessary. Here lies the real risk for the U.S. Force is forever the servant of Communist policies. It will be used not only on the defensive occasion but also to further the success of the offensive move.

Therefore the U.S. must always expect from the Soviet Union the threat, and the use of apt force in support of declared policies. This, I repeat, is the real risk, the ever present likelihood—in fact, the certainty—to which American policy must address itself. This risk was disregarded by the sweeping three-part disarmament policy set by the U.S. in 1956. My proposal takes it fully into account.

For the rest, there remains the outside possibility, the unlikely contingency, the tenuous risk that no disarmament policy, however ingenious, can absolutely exclude. Might it not happen that, at some future and undetermined date, in a conjectural situation of possible Communist nuclear superiority, the Soviet Union might conceivably threaten the use of total nuclear violence, for no very clear or predictable political purpose? Who could possibly answer this question? This is not the kind of guesswork on which present American policy ought to be based. For my part, I cherish the confident hope that, if such a threat of violence were ever to be made, the United States would be secure enough in other forms of valid nuclear strength, to have the courage simply to defy it.

Let us, however, come back from speculations about the unforeseeable future to the certain and seen realities of the present. The existent fact is that the real invitation to military helplessness and political defeat before the advancing forces of communism is being issued by the present rigidity of the American posture, both political and military, that refuses to make the essential distinction between apt force and inept violence. The enforcement of this distinction points the only way to security, both for ourselves and for all the world.

I do not, of course, maintain that it will be easy to negotiate in detail the precise and concrete meaning of this distinction as applied to nuclear stockpiles. But I do maintain that this is the cardinal issue that needs to be negotiated. I further maintain that the necessary premise of negotiation exists. It is a matter of self-interest to both parties to agree to the distinction itself and to strike a further agreement to negotiate its practical meaning. Success in the negotiations is not assured. But at least success is a more genuine possibility and a more instant necessity in this area than anywhere else.

Nor need we fear that the guidance of Divine Providence will be lacking to us as we thus set to work to dismantle the Era of Terror, which has grown increasingly offensive to the moral conscience. The redemption of mankind from the dominion of terror is not alien to the intentions of God.

DISARMAMENT IN THE NUCLEAR AGE [5]

HUBERT H. HUMPHREY [6]

An uncommonly well-informed man, Senator Humphrey (Democrat, Minnesota) speaks out of wide experience in practical politics and close observation of the national and international scene. Referring to Humphrey, Cabell Phillips, Washington correspondent of the New York *Times* Sunday department, said: "Politics of the familiar, orthodox variety runs through his veins like blood." He is a tireless worker and indeed one of the most vigorous, dynamic speakers in public life.

A member of the powerful Committee on Foreign Relations of the United States Senate, Humphrey has been deeply concerned over the alleged failure of the executive branch of the government to formulate an "established policy" on disarmament. Accordingly, he has set forth proposals for strengthening America's hand in the disarmament conferences. Even more importantly, however, he has urged the Government to come up with a plan. As he put it in a short statement to the Senate on January 27, 1960: "I implore this administration to wake up, to start moving, and to get on with the task of developing a coherent, effective, imaginative policy for the control and reduction of the world's armaments."

The following is one of several speeches which he has given on the theme of disarmament. It was delivered at Yale University on December 6, 1959.

Disarmament should be the core of American foreign policy. We are a nation dedicated to peace and we know that peace is always threatened by an arms race. A case can be built for an armament structure as a holding action, but a world armed to the teeth is a dangerous world. Progress on controlling arms is urgently needed so that the people of all nations may devote their full talents and energies to peaceful and constructive pursuits. The control and reduction of armaments is an immensely difficult problem. I have chosen this evening to discuss certain of its aspects and to put before you a program for the future.

[5] Text furnished by Senator Humphrey, with permission for this reprint.

[6] For biographical note, see Appendix; for reference to an earlier speech, see Cumulative Author Index.

During the early part of this year's session of the United Nations General Assembly, Premier Khrushchev spoke on the subject of disarmament. He made some rather sweeping proposals including a proposal for total disarmament in four years. The Soviet Union was not the only country to offer disarmament proposals before the UN. The British advanced an equally comprehensive scheme for substantial cutback in armaments in stages. The Irish submitted a resolution to bar the transfer of nuclear weapons from nuclear powers to nonnuclear. A resolution, adopted by the UN General Assembly, and sponsored by a large group of nations in Asia and Africa, called on the French to call off their scheduled atomic tests in the Sahara.

The significance of this activity in the United Nations, to me, is two-fold. First, the question of disarmament, or arms control to use a broader phrase, is mounting in interest and intensity throughout the world. Second, it was most unfortunate that in all of this debate and discussion, the United States was on the sidelines because we did not have any concrete proposals of our own to advocate. Our position throughout the debate was confined to one of assuring UN members that our policy is under review and that all proposals of other nations should be submitted to the forthcoming disarmament negotiations between five Western nations and five Soviet bloc nations.

My complaint is not that we told the UN that we were studying the matter. My criticism is that such a position was far from adequate—a far cry from the position the leader of the free world should be prepared to take on one of the most vital issues facing the world at this time.

The most recent over-all position of the United States on the broad subject of disarmament was stated in August, 1957. Yet the Administration waited until August of 1959 before appointing a group to review the policy to determine what we should seek in 1960.

Our policy should be under constant scrutiny all the time. But to say we are reviewing past policy on arms control puts the matter in the wrong perspective. It is not enough to review what has gone before. What is urgently needed is a policy for the future, one that can be used as a basis for discussion and negotiations. A policy that states goals and the concrete steps to realize the goals is what the world wants to hear from the United States.

Progress toward any kind of arms control requires infinite patience. But there is a difference between the patience that is based on planning and prodding and the patience of procrastination, timidity and indecision.

The President in a letter to me of November 17, did reaffirm his belief in the need for progress on disarmament. I commend the President for his statement of purpose. Too bad so many of his advisers fail to share his aims and vision. Although it is belated, it is encouraging that the President has begun to see that goals, in order to be translated into specific steps, demand preparation, study and even funds.

Progress on arms control can be made. But it takes the kind of stubborn concentration of people who refuse to give up at the first signs of delay or the first obstacles to progress.

During the recent session of Congress I tried on four different appropriation bills to get $400,000 earmarked for disarmament studies. Each time the Administration failed to give support. Regrettably, the Congress failed also.

Next year I shall try again. The Department of State has indicated that it will recommend funds for arms control preparation and studies.

Nuclear Test Ban Agreement Closer

Today, I offer three arms control proposals which should be given the highest priority. In proposing them I am assuming there will be continued negotiations for a ban on nuclear weapons tests. I give the test ban talks a better than even chance of being successful. I believe the outcome will be based on a control system for the cessation of all atomic tests, initiated perhaps in stages and possibly along the lines I recently outlined in an address at Pontiac, Michigan.

Many people within the Administration have fought the concept of a comprehensive and controlled test ban agreement. They have fought it all year and they are still fighting it. I was sorry to note opponents of a test ban seem to have recruited Governor Rockefeller to their side. Whether Vice President Nixon is there too no one can be sure. The political wind evidently is not yet strong enough for him to tell which way it is going and, therefore, which direction he should likewise go.

One of the ways test ban opponents try to scuttle an agreement is to call for a control and inspection system that is 100 per cent perfect. The AEC and the Pentagon know themselves that perfection in an arms control system is no more possible than perfection in an early warning radar system against surprise attack or perfection in the safety precautions taken to prevent radioactivity from escaping from a nuclear reactor.

The President has now begun to shake up his subordinates on this matter. In his November 17 letter to me he said:

> The best and most carefully elaborated disarmament agreements are likely to carry with them some risks, at least theoretically, of evasion. But one must ponder, in reaching decisions on the very complex and difficult subject of arms control, the enormous risks entailed if reasonable steps are not taken to curb the international competition in armaments and to move effectively in the direction of disarmament.

The President is right. There are risks in the failure to act, just as there are risks in carefully designed action.

With continued and concentrated bargaining and perseverance a test ban agreement may be reached within the next several months. The President wants a test ban agreement before he leaves office and the Russians seem to want to limit the nuclear club. The votes in the UN General Assembly indicate world opinion insists upon a test ban. I am convinced the people of the United States want the tests stopped. They want to make a start on controlling the arms race. When Governor Rockefeller made his unfortunate, and in my opinion, misguided statement over TV on resuming underground tests, the TV studio was besieged with calls of protest.

But we must prepare to go beyond a controlled and inspected nuclear weapons test. This merely opens the door to genuine disarmament. We should make a concerted attack on three major problems in the arms control field.

Goals to Work Toward

Let me make it clear I stand for a world free from the burden of massive armaments. I support the goal of a United Nations police force equipped to guard all nations, large and small, from aggression. I am for a system of world order in which law takes the place of force as a means of settling disputes. And I believe that eventually the nations of the world must agree to view any act of an individual, group or nation that seeks to disturb world peace as a crime against mankind. Specific steps now must be taken to assure the ultimate fulfillment of these long-range goals.

Defense Must Be Maintained Until Disarmament Is Reached

The proposals I offer are all based on the concept of mutual agreement. I do not support unilateral disarmament. We have already had too much of this in the name of a balanced budget. Until we have concrete progress in arms control our own defense posture must not only be maintained but even strengthened in key respects.

Now my proposals.

No. 1. Control and reduction of missiles and bombers and maintenance of outer space for peaceful purposes.

We must seek the control and reduction of long-range missiles and long-range bombers. We must increase our efforts to preserve outer space for peaceful purposes.

The universe waits to be explored and understood. The nations of the earth must together seek knowledge about the unknown. They must simultaneously develop a law of conduct in the universe if peaceful undertakings are not to be turned into warfare. Insofar as we possibly can, therefore, the delivery vehicles of warfare should be controlled and curtailed. Of these the most important are the missiles and then the bombers.

This means inspectors and control posts located at every strategic air base. Inspectors and control posts will need to be established near the launching sites for missiles as well as aboard every naval vessel equipped for missile launchings.

But control is not enough. The missiles and bombers must either be eliminated or they must be placed under international control. Further tests of missiles under such a system would be prohibited and a monitoring system installed to see that they were, in fact, stopped.

Such a program as this cannot be accomplished overnight. Long-range missile and bomber control is an enormously difficult problem. I am told, for example, that enough missiles might be launched from one site to effect a major knock-out blow. A control system for missiles and bombers involving bases and launching sites throughout the world would be far more difficult to negotiate than a ban on nuclear weapons tests. Therefore, studies on control measures should be begun immediately. They should be started at home, internally by the U.S., and also joint talks should be proposed with the Soviet Union and other powers that would be affected. The studies might first be conducted on a technical level prior to political negotiations.

For years we have talked about the threat of the nuclear delivery systems. The talk must now be translated into action.

No. 2. Cessation of nuclear weapons production.

The production of fissionable material for weapons purposes should be curtailed under effective safeguards.

Here again there has been a lot of talk but little action. We need first to work out, preferably jointly with the Soviet Union and Great Britain, the necessary technical means of control. We need a control system adequate to prevent the secret diversion of fissionable materials from peaceful pursuits to weapons purposes. This control system should be adequate but not more than is required. The last estimate I have seen given by the AEC for such a control system involved about 5,000 inspectors in the

Soviet Union. I cannot judge at this point whether this is necessary. It appears to me rather high considering that the test ban control system for the USSR would involve far less than 1,000 inspectors.

A controlled ban on the production of nuclear weapons would affect not only the three nuclear powers. It would also stop other nations from arming themselves with their own nuclear weapons. The French, for example, have said repeatedly they would give up their plans to test and produce nuclear weapons if other nations stopped their nuclear weapons production. A control system for the prohibition of nuclear weapons production might be fitted into the functions of the International Atomic Energy Agency.

No. 3. World-wide multi-nation system against surprise attack.

We need a world-wide anti-surprise attack system against the use of any kind of military force by one country against another.

The term, surprise attack, has come to mean within the United States, primarily an attack by long-range missiles and aircraft. This does not include all that I mean. The problem is not solely one of missiles and bombers nor of the three nuclear powers. It includes surprise attack by Chinese Communists on India, Nepal, Burma, Laos, Korea, or Formosa. It concerns a possible aggression in the Middle East. It concerns a possible aggression in Central and Eastern Europe. And finally it even concerns possible aggression in Latin America.

A focus on the prevention of this kind of surprise attack is essential and urgent for two major reasons. First, it is important because most of the real threats of warfare come from the kinds of situations I have mentioned. Every time a local or regional war breaks out it threatens to drag in the major powers with their large-scale and devastating weapons.

Second, it is important because if the nuclear powers place under control and limit their missiles, bombers, and fissionable material for weapons purposes this might give other powers the idea they can afford to become more reckless. In other words, the possession of weapons of mass destruction has acted to some extent as a deterrent on non-nuclear powers as well as nuclear. No nation can be sure that what it hopes may be a small war won't turn into a world-wide catastrophe. If the big weapons were controlled or removed, some irresponsible dictator with heavy conventional armaments somewhere might feel the risk of aggression was not too great. Until you have assurance of protection from surprise attack you have an unstable world situation where the finger is never far from the trigger.

An anti-surprise attack system should include many elements. In some areas the withdrawal or pullback of troops would be called for. In other areas a controlled demilitarized zone would be needed. Still other areas might require the stationing of an international police force. Special inspection posts would need to be established in all areas. The UN would truly become the eyes and ears of peace.

You may think this sounds like a lot of inspection and inspectors. It would be. But it is necessary to have what each situation demands.

Importance of Inspection for a Peaceful World

In our country I think we believe inspection and control are necessary because we don't trust the Russians. This is certainly an element but this is not the entire explanation. It is deeper than that.

Inspection and control recognize something about human nature. It recognizes that man is not perfect.

If controls and regulations are needed in a well-organized national society, and they certainly are, they are even more important in relations among nation states.

Americans are a peace-loving, honest and just people. The overwhelming majority of us want to obey the law, do well unto others, and avoid harm wherever and whenever we can. Yet we have dotted our society from stem to stern inside and out with inspectors. Just let me list for you some of the ways we inspect each other.

At the Federal level we have inspectors for a multitude of purposes:

Food and Drug inspectors
Coast Guard inspectors
Narcotics inspectors
The Customs Service
The Secret Service
FBI agents
Civil Service investigators
Atomic Energy inspectors

In the armed services we have a military police system that consists of 23,976 Army police; 2,407 Navy police; and 34,894 Air Force police.

And in the internal revenue service we have inspectors in the thousands including a couple of hundred to inspect the inspectors.

James Madison said many years ago: "If men were angels, no government would be necessary. If angels were to govern men, neither external nor internal controls on government would be necessary." It goes without saying, I think, that international relations are not conducted by angels either.

Inspection, therefore, is highly essential for a peaceful world as well as a just and functioning society. The sooner we start detailed studies and negotiations combining inspection and control with the reduction of armaments and the prevention of surprise attack the sooner we may reach our goal.

I cannot emphasize too strongly the need to get started. We are going into our third year of serious discussion for a test ban. Each of the three fields I have mentioned may take at least that long to show progress.

Regional Disarmament Conferences Needed

These three proposals cannot be negotiated by the same people at the same conference. The missile-bomber problem and the cut-off of fissionable material for weapons purposes can be undertaken primarily by the nuclear powers with assistance from others. But separate conferences will be necessary. It will be necessary to initiate regional conferences to handle the creation of anti-surprise attack systems in the different areas of the world.

What I am suggesting here is that the ten-nation disarmament negotiations to be convened early next year can only make a start on the problem. They will not be able in one conference to settle the problems I have discussed here as well as others that also must be tackled. Perhaps the greatest contribution the forthcoming ten-nation disarmament conference can make is to undertake serious negotiations for a system to prevent surprise attack in Europe.

Other Arms Control Problems

As I have advanced my three major proposals many of you may have been thinking about still other problems. We are all aware of many other areas on which work must be done. In the arms control field there are weapons of bacteriological and chemical warfare. There are the armed forces of nations. There are the delivery vehicles other than missiles and bombers. In the matter of prevention of aggression there is the overriding problem of settling the disputes and removing the friction among nations that lead to aggression. And there is the special problem of China.

All of these matters require thought, study, and action. But I submit we must make a start. I have chosen three areas that are particularly important.

The Special Problem of China

Now, before closing, a word about China. The Communist government of China would have to be bound by any arms control system that dealt effectively with missiles and bombers and the prevention of surprise attack. Without China no system for the prevention of surprise attack in eastern and southern Asia could be successful. Without China in an arms control agreement affecting Asia, the entire power balance in the world could be dangerously upset. National security and world security demand the inclusion of Communist China in major arms control agreements.

Unfortunately, Communist China is still highly irresponsible and aggressive. It may take the combined persuasiveness of the Soviet Union, the United States, and all the countries of Asia to impress on China the need to forgo plans of aggression and defiance of the international community. Strange as it may seem to think of U.S.-Soviet cooperation on persuading China to participate in a disarmament agreement, the world situation may yet produce such a result.

We are entering a period in which the subject of arms reduction and control is taking on new meaning. There are dangers as well as opportunities. But the goal of a peaceful world demands our best efforts.

And the goal of peace must not be a sterile and cold concept meaning merely the absence of war or hostilities. It is a peace with justice and opportunity, better living conditions, education and health for all mankind. Peace is not slogans but programs. This kind of peace is not easy; it is sacrifice. Peace requires more than public relations. It demands a continuity and depth of public policy. My wish is that my program of disarmament offered here tonight will help to stimulate and inspire others.

REFLECTIONS ON CONTINUING RESPONSIBILITIES

NEW DIRECTIONS FOR FOREIGN AID [1]

CHESTER BOWLES [2]

In his message to Congress on January 6, 1941, Franklin D. Roosevelt said:

> I also ask this Congress for authority and for funds sufficient to manufacture additional munitions and war supplies of many kinds, to be turned over to those nations which are now in actual war with aggressor nations. Our most useful and immediate role is to act as an arsenal for them as well as for ourselves. They do not need manpower, but they do need billions of dollars' worth of the weapons of defense.
>
> The time is near when they will not be able to pay for them all in ready cash. We cannot, and we will not, tell them that they must surrender merely because of present inability to pay for the weapons which we know they must have.
>
> For what we send abroad we shall be repaid, repaid within a reasonable time following the close of hostilities, repaid in similar materials, or at our option in other goods of many kinds which they can produce and which we need.

The "lend-lease" idea took deep roots. For nearly twenty years, "foreign aid"—under a variety of terms—has played an important role in the foreign policy of the United States.

In September 1959, Congress authorized slightly more than $3.2 billion for the mutual security program, some $750 million less than the Administration requested. For the fiscal year 1961, the President asked for $4.1 billion to cover the costs of military and economic aid. Critics of the program repeatedly questioned both the total outlay and the usefulness of the plan. The debate continued.

One of our most knowledgeable men on the operation and effectiveness of the foreign aid program is Chester Bowles, Democratic congressman from Connecticut. Actively associated with aid programs for nearly fifteen years, he brings to the discussion of the subject an unusual ex-

---

[1] Text furnished by Representative Bowles, with permission for this reprint.

[2] For biographical note, see Appendix; for reference to an earlier speech, see Cumulative Author Index.

perience, keen insight, and a temperate wisdom commanding respect.

The speech was delivered in the House of Representatives on April 20, 1959. A similar though somewhat longer report on the theme made up his Edmund Walsh lecture at Georgetown University on March 11, 1959.

Mr. Speaker, few subjects on the minds of the American people and the agenda of Congress are as important as foreign aid. And probably on no subject is there so much disagreement, misunderstanding, and frustration.

There have always been a number of hard-core opponents of foreign aid in the Congress. This year, as in the past, they will oppose the mutual security bill with vigor and skill.

What I find much more disturbing is the opposition of old friends of the program who are deeply concerned over the direction in which it has been moving.

When we add the frustration in this body created by threats of presidential vetoes of such domestic programs as schools, area development, housing, and urban renewal—programs which many of us believe to be essential to the well-being of our own country —the danger of deep and dangerous retaliatory cuts in foreign aid becomes apparent.

Mr. Speaker, I believe that those of us who have supported this program from the beginning, and who believe that it is even more vitally needed today, have a special responsibility to explore the reasons for the present confusion and opposition and to propose positive steps that Congress can take to help clear the air.

I speak as such a supporter, who intends to vote for the full amount requested by the President.

I also speak from fourteen years of varied experience in the planning and administrating of foreign aid programs both for the United Nations and our own Government.

As the U.S. Stabilization Director at the war's end, I was concerned with the planning of our relief food shipments to Europe and Asia.

As a U.S. delegate to the first UNESCO Conference in Paris in 1946, I participated in planning the initial programs of this new agency.

As special consultant to the Secretary General of the United Nations in 1947 and 1948, I surveyed and reported on United Nations child welfare assistance programs in France, Italy, Poland, Hungary, and Czechoslovakia.

As U.S. Ambassador to India and Nepal in 1951-53, I had direct responsibility for staffing, planning, and administering our own first major Point Four effort. This included the launching of the world's first major community development program, a program that now embraces 320,000 Indian villages and 180 million people.

Since leaving India, Mr. Speaker, I have had continuing first-hand opportunities to study American and United Nations aid programs in Pakistan, Afghanistan, Vietnam, Burma, Indonesia, Thailand, Formosa, Korea, the Philippines, Ethiopia, and in several African countries and territories south of the Sahara.

I have seen the near miracles that can be accomplished in the villages when the right amount of technical assistance is fruitfully combined with small amounts of capital and the active, energetic participation of the local inhabitants.

I have seen the democratic lift, purpose, and pride that new industries, improved transportation, and expanding hydroelectric power can give to old societies.

I have also seen what can happen in terms of waste and frustration when American aid is spent in the wrong place, in the wrong way, and for the wrong reasons.

Experiences of this kind are bound to give any observer a profound awareness of the enormous complexities with which our foreign aid administrators must contend day after day. Intricate and delicate problems must be weighed and balanced. Assorted pressures of many kinds require the utmost in tact and perseverance.

May I add that my criticisms are not intended for any individual. I have developed the greatest respect and admiration for many of the hard-working and dedicated public servants who have administered our aid programs through the years. Mr. C. Douglas Dillon, Under Secretary of State, who now has general supervision over these programs, in particular is a man of unique competence and ability.

The fact remains that errors of omission and commission in our foreign aid programs are substantial and they have been well publicized. No doubt they will again be stressed with vigor in the coming debates.

Yet when our oratory has died away, this over-all aid effort will remain absolutely and urgently essential to America's immediate and long-range interests and to our hopes of building a lasting peace. We simply cannot afford to carve up the aid program; much less can we afford to abandon it.

What we must do is to introduce standards that will help assure more realistic planning and administration, and at the same time frankly explain to the American people why foreign aid is needed, what it can do, and, equally important, what it cannot do.

Ultimately, Mr. Speaker, we shall need a better balance among various aid programs and perhaps additional international machinery. I merely refer in passing to certain developments which I should like to see happen but which I shall not discuss today.

For instance, I would prefer that a larger proportion of our technical assistance be channeled through the United Nations technical assistance program than is presently the case.

I would like to see Senator Monroney's proposal for an international development association given more serious consideration.

In our own mutual security program I would feel happier if we could separate economic from military assistance completely.

Finally, I would advocate more emphasis on long-term loan commitments to encourage more efficient planning and to discourage waste.

No man with a realistic appreciation of the circumstances of the moment, both in the Administration and in the Congress, will feel there is a possibility for major thoroughgoing revision of the mutual security legislation this year.

Most of the suggestions I have just mentioned are unlikely to receive effective consideration during the present session of Congress. But this does not mean that we are powerless between now and adjournment to compel less expediency, less waste, less confusion, and, consequently, better performance.

As a contribution to this essential, immediate strengthening of the program, I suggest the following four changes in the present legislation, which I believe it would be practicable to make in the mutual security authorization legislation this year:

First. A revised statement of the purposes of our aid legislation, which more positively reflects America's true, long-range objectives in world affairs.

Second. A set of standards that will help channel military assistance to those nations which have genuine need for such assistance to deter Communist aggression, and which will discourage arms shipments to countries where such shipments lead to internal instability and regional conflicts.

Third. A set of standards which will give high priority for technical assistance and development loans to nations which will demonstrate a willingness to sacrifice in their own behalf and whose governments are so organized that they can use our help with a minimum of waste.

Fourth. An increase in the Development Loan Fund to $1 billion annually. The additional $300 million can, I believe, be saved by a reasonable application of the standards I have suggested above.

I. Needed: A New Statement of Purpose

Mr. Speaker, I shall explain as briefly as I can the reasons for each of these proposals.

One of the principal reasons why we now face grave difficulties in securing adequate funds for foreign aid is the failure of the Administration to explain honestly and frankly why it is so urgently needed.

Thus a reluctant Congress has been asked each year to support this effort for a variety of expedient reasons calculated to frighten or woo us into favorable, last-minute, emergency action.

Because many of these official reasons have turned out to be superficial and unrealistic, the American people have become increasingly confused and the Congress increasingly impatient.

I know of no greater tribute to our national intelligence than the public opinion polls which consistently show that nearly 70 per cent of all Americans strongly support the foreign aid program in spite of their government's failure to spell out its true, long-range objectives.

The official purposes which are now most often advanced for foreign aid are inadequate for several reasons.

They fail to do justice to America's real goals in world affairs.

They fail to appeal to the common concern for the dignity of man which we share with people all over the non-Communist world.

And they fail to take into account the intelligence and decency of the American people themselves.

The preamble to the Mutual Security Act now implies that it it is "the policy of the United States to continue" the aid program only "as long as (the Communist) danger . . . persists."

Thus, for purposes of qualifying for American dollars, we have officially turned communism into a natural resource like oil or uranium. In the marketplace of the cold war, a noisy Communist minority has become worth its weight in gold.

The apocryphal account of a Monacan foreign minister's visit to Washington to secure $10 million in aid is well known in every world capital.

The arrangement was ready to be signed and sealed, so the story goes, when the American negotiator turned to the Monacan official and casually remarked: "I understand you have been having fearful trouble recently with your Communist agitators."

The foreign minister proudly replied that Monaco was almost free of Communists. The startled American official shook his head sadly. "Congress," he said, "will never stand for a grant of $10 million to a country with no Communists."

The disheartened Monacan official returned home by way of Paris and, as a last resort, called on the French foreign minister. After explaining his predicament, he asked if it might not be possible to borrow a few angry, window-breaking French Communists to help bolster Monaco's application for American aid.

His French counterpart looked at him soberly. "My friend," he finally said, "I am afraid we must refuse. Although France is anxious to be a good neighbor, we need every single Communist that we have."

As long as the preamble of the Mutual Security Act reads as it now reads, Communist agitators may logically say to their Asian, African, and Latin American audiences: "The Soviet Union offers you loans and technicians to speed your economic developments. For this you are grateful.

"But should you not be equally grateful to Moscow for the aid you get from Washington?

"In their own official statement of purpose at the beginning of their mutual security legislation, the Americans frankly state that if they were not so frightened of us Communists, they would give you nothing."

Another supporting reason for the foreign aid program, which is often officially offered in discreet, off-the-record talks, is its alleged usefulness in buying majority support for our policies in the United Nations General Assembly.

But Mr. Speaker, is this second reason any more valid than the first?

Suppose a wealthy man came to live in a typical American community to finance a series of community improvements in return for public acceptance of his political views. Would not most upstanding, civic-minded people urge him to take his bene-factions elsewhere?

Can we expect the proud new nations of Asia and Africa, and the older nations of Europe and Latin America to react differently?

A third mistaken argument for foreign assistance is that communism appeals only to hungry people. "Just fill everyone's stomach with rice," we sometimes hear, "and that will be the end of communism in the underdeveloped world."

This view reflects a massive lack of understanding of the Communist appeal and indeed of human nature. Frustrations which grow from injustice and the absence of a sense of belonging are far stronger motivations toward communism than pure hunger.

Indeed, if an Asian, African, or Latin American government is content to give its people food while refusing them the right to till their own land and to work democratically with their neighbors in creating better communities, the government may end up with a better fed, and therefore more dangerous, Communist minority than it had in the first place.

The objectives of American assistance have not always been advanced in such negative terms.

Consider, for instance, the breadth and vision of President Roosevelt's eloquent appeal to Congress and the American people in behalf of lend-lease in 1941, of Secretary Marshall's historic speech in 1947 at Harvard boldly spelling out the partnership relationships of the Marshall plan, of President Truman's Point Four statement in his 1949 inaugural message proposing economic aid and technical assistance to the new underdeveloped nations.

In each case the objectives were magnificently positive, practical, and within our democratic tradition.

Nor did we rely alone on the eloquence of our presidents and secretaries of state to present America's true objectives to the world.

Year after year the Congress of the United States specifically wrote them into the preambles and statements of purpose of our foreign aid legislation.

For example, in the Foreign Assistance Act of 1948 the Eightieth Congress called for steps designed to strengthen "the principles of individual liberty, free institutions, and genuine independence, based upon a strong production effort, the expansion of foreign trade, the creation and maintenance of internal financial stability, and the development of economic cooperation."

In the Foreign Economic Assistance Act of 1950 the Eighty-first Congress said:

The peoples of the United States and other nations have a common interest in the freedom and in the economic and social progress of all peoples.

The efforts of the peoples living in economically underdeveloped areas of the world to realize their full capabilities and to develop the resources of the lands in which they live can be furthered through the cooperative endeavor of all nations to exchange technical knowledge and skills and to encourage the flow of investment capital.

It is declared to be the policy of the United States to aid the efforts of the peoples of economically underdeveloped areas to develop their resources and improve their working and living conditions by encouraging the exchange of technical knowledge and skills and the flow of investment capital to countries which provide conditions under which such technical assistance and capital can effectively and constructively contribute to raising standards of living, creating new sources of wealth, increasing productivity, and expanding purchasing power.

It is further declared to be the policy of the United States that in order to achieve the most effective utilization of the resources of the United States, private and public, which are or may be available for aid in the development of economically underdeveloped areas, agencies of the U.S. Government, in reviewing requests of foreign governments for aid for such purposes, shall take into consideration whether the assistance applied for is an appropriate part of a program reasonably designed to contribute to the balanced and integrated development of the country or area concerned.

Against this background, Mr. Speaker, the 1954 statement of purpose retained in this year's bill, appears unworthy of us. Its implied motivations are negative, expedient, and unrealistic.

In this critical period in history, I believe we should stop underestimating the American people. It is time to put aside the sales gimmicks and to do what needs to be done for the right reasons.

Why Is Foreign Aid Really Needed?

The reasons why the mutual security legislation is essential to America's objectives can be simply stated:

In the last fifteen years a political and economic revolution of extraordinary dimensions has swept Asia, Africa, and Latin America.

Seven hundred million people have won their freedom from colonial rule. In spite of lack of capital, of technicians, and of administrative skills, they and their contemporaries in other underdeveloped nations are now working impatiently to grow more food, create new industries, and build a better future for their people.

The resulting situation is politically explosive for two reasons:

First. The utter poverty and slow pace of change in much of Asia, Africa, and of Latin America, contrasts sharply with the extraordinary wealth and economic growth of the privileged peoples of Western Europe, Canada, and the United States. This creates envy and frustration.

Second. Communism now offers the underdeveloped continents, not only the glittering Soviet example of a modern industrial nation created out of chaos in two generations, but substantial capital and large numbers of skilled technicians with which to make a similar transition. This offers harried new nationalist leaders a tempting shortcut.

Is it surprising, Mr. Speaker, to find the Soviet leaders now fishing in the politically troubled waters of Asia, Africa, and Latin America with such effectiveness?

The Kremlin's primary objective in its efforts toward world domination is to split the Western world with its 600 million highly skilled and industrialized people. This calls for the ultimate separation of Western Europe from America.

For nearly a generation the Soviet Union has been pursuing this objective by two different but related tactics.

First. Direct action against our NATO alliance such as the effort made in the late 1940's and in the present Soviet-generated crisis over Berlin.

Second. A flanking attack through the churning continents of Asia, Africa, and Latin America which contain the raw materials on which Europe's prosperity depends and where revolutionary change is now the order of the day.

Forty years ago Lenin said, "The road to Paris lies through Calcutta and Peiping." He believed that control over a sizable fraction of the resources of these rich continents would enable the world Communist movement eventually to break the back of heavily industrialized Europe.

Fortunately for the world Stalin lacked the capital, technicians, and understanding of peasant Asia to follow this approach effectively. But Khrushchev has the resources and the astuteness that Stalin lacked, and he is now using them both with vigor and skill.

We have no desire to control the nations or the resources of Asia, Africa, and Latin America. We seek no satellites. We have no wish to impose our ways on others.

Indeed our own nation was born in revolution and since our earliest days we have associated ourselves with the efforts of people everywhere to gain and maintain their freedom, and to create their own futures in their own way.

Thomas Jefferson once said that the "American Revolution is intended for all mankind."

Tom Paine spoke of the small spark kindled in America that could never be extinguished.

George Washington believed that the freedom of the world was "finally staked on the experiment attributed to the American people" and remarked that he felt "irresistibly excited whenever in any country I see an oppressed people unfurl the banner of freedom."

The American Revolution, Abraham Lincoln said, would eventually ease the lot of people on a great portion of the globe.

Moreover, America's role of leader in mankind's struggle for freedom was accepted and understood far beyond our shores. As he watched the new countries of Latin America throw off colonial rule with American assistance after the Napoleonic wars, Austrian Foreign Minister Metternich complained that America is constantly "fostering revolutions wherever they show themselves, regretting those that fail, and extending a helping hand to those which succeed."

Our major purpose now as then is to encourage free peoples to stand on their own feet, to make their own choices, to defend themselves against overt aggression, and to create economic and political conditions under which the principles of liberty and human dignity can take root, grow, and ultimately flourish.

Our global objective remains what it was in Jefferson's time: a world of peace in which all men may have the opportunity to develop freely and independently within the framework of their own cultures, religions, and national capabilities.

That, Mr. Speaker, is why we need the Mutual Security Act now and that is why we will continue to need similar legislation for many years to come.

The time has come to give the American people and the world a positive indication that the objectives of our mutual security program are worthy of our historic political convictions and of our democratic beliefs.

In the absence of strong Administration leadership, the Congress cannot rewrite our foreign aid program as I believe it should be rewritten. But we can, if we will, give the program an identity and purpose that not only fits the urgency and the nature of our times but which also reflects the true, long-range, global objectives of the American people.

Mr. Speaker, my first proposal in regard to this year's mutual security bill is that we clearly spell out these objectives. I have indicated the directions in which such new language should point.

II. Who Should Have Military Aid?

Mr. Speaker, I shall now turn to my second proposed change.

I am impatient, and I believe others here are too, with the present wasteful, and often ineffective, methods of allocating some of our military assistance. In many cases we have inadvertently created situations which have played into the hands of the Communists and increased their influence.

I realize, of course, that in certain areas which are clearly threatened by Communist aggression, military considerations often must take precedence, at least for the short haul. Western Europe, Greece, Turkey, Yugoslavia, Korea, Formosa, and Vietnam, are all cases in point. Here substantial American military assistance remains absolutely essential.

But in two whole continents—South America and Africa, and in much of the vast arc of Asia that stretches from Lebanon to Manila—the principal threat to world peace comes not from Soviet tanks and jets but from economic strangulation, injustice, and human frustration.

In these areas, haphazard shipments of American military equipment seldom coincide with our long-term security interests, much less with those of the people in the country concerned.

Such military assistance given on an expedient basis is almost invariably self-defeating. It adds to internal economic strains. It diverts internal efforts from constructive development. It paves the way for palace revolutions. In some cases it ties our prestige and our influence to the dubious tenure of dictatorships which are sooner or later destined to be swept aside.

Military assistance injected into these surging continents may be particularly harmful if it is given without proper regard for regional political considerations. By disrupting the delicate balance of power between a recipient nation and its non-Communist neighbors, indiscriminate arms shipments jeopardize the military and political stability of the entire area.

Internal economic factors must also be taken into account. I know of no more effective way to undermine a wobbly new government than to burden it unnecessarily with an excessive military load that prevents its leaders from focusing their attention on essential tasks like growing rice, driving out malaria and building schools, clinics, and roads.

The more arms we pour into such situations, the more we inflate the power of the military, the easier it is for ambitious officers to seize power and the further we stray from our essential democratic purposes.

Mr. Speaker, for all of these reasons, I believe it is essential that we reconsider on a country-by-country basis the effectiveness of our military assistance program.

We must determine precisely where we are heading with our military aid programs in Asia, Africa, and Latin America and establish more realistic standards for the granting of such assistance.

I do not propose that we recklessly repudiate old arrangements. But I believe we should insist that they be shaped to new objectives and that new agreements which fail to meet these standards should be ruled out.

III. Standards for Economic Aid

Let me now consider, Mr. Speaker, the need for a more realistic approach to the distribution of economic assistance.

Why is it that a dam can be built and operated with great success in one country, while in another country a similar dam is a miserable failure?

Why is it that modern equipment can make a vital contribution to increasing agricultural and small industrial productivity in the villages of some countries while similar machinery sent to other countries lies rusting on the docks?

In most cases it reflects basic differences between the countries and the governments in question—differences which we have often lamentably failed to take into account.

The underdeveloped countries of the world fall into many categories.

The most favorable opportunities for American assistance exist in those countries which are not only determined to build solid economic and social foundations, but which also have the built-in capacity to implement their plans.

In such countries, which unhappily are too few in number, we should be prepared to make bolder and longer term investments of our capital and our skills.

At the other extreme are those nations which, because of lack of leadership, of administrative experience, or of courage to put through essential reforms, are clearly incapable of meeting the minimum practical requirements of rapid economic development under present conditions.

In such countries, experience demonstrates that long-term loans or investment grants for general economic development are wasteful and foolhardy.

Any effort to force the pace beyond their capacity to use the funds effectively will almost certainly fail, and failure will lead to frustration on our part and bitterness on theirs.

Between these extremes there are many variations which will require judgment and understanding.

Mr. Speaker, I suggest the following five standards to measure the capacity of each country to use our long-term economic development assistance. I believe they are both practical and urgently necessary.

Five Standards for Judgment

First. The most important standard for granting American economic loans and other assistance should be that of self-sacrifice.

To become eligible for substantial long-term assistance, a nation should demonstrate that it is making a substantial effort to finance its own national development from its own resources.

Evidence of this willingness for self-sacrifice should include a reasonably effective program of national taxation based on individual ability to pay, controls over the importation of luxuries and nonessentials which otherwise rapidly eat up foreign exchange, and a determined and continuing effort to assure the maximum number of peasant families ownership of their own land.

Second. To qualify for major American investment assistance, an underdeveloped nation should have put together a practical, comprehensive set of economic objectives and itemized the allocation of all available resources to achieve those objectives.

This assures that important tasks will be given priority, that the development program will be relevantly related to private and public income, and that the need for international help will be more accurately assessed.

If there is already a significant private business sector, it should be considered side by side in such a plan with government-sponsored agricultural power and transportation projects in formulating the national development scheme.

Third. A qualifying country should have a reasonably substantial, competent, and graft-free civil service. Without able technicians, tax collectors, and administrators, large amounts of investment capital cannot be used to economic advantage.

Fourth. In order to qualify for long-term investment assistance, a country should also have a relatively stable government with popular roots.

Our democratic tradition makes most Americans unsympathetic to authoritarian governments of whatever persuasion. But this does not mean, Mr. Speaker, that our aid should be restricted to parliamentary democracies modeled on the West.

Indeed, we must face the fact that most of the new nations of Asia and Africa, over the long haul, may consider our own institutions unsuitable. Of these the least likely to succeed are those whose power is based on the shifting loyalties of feudal landlords and money-lenders.

By forgoing the support of both the middle-class center and the non-Communist left, such governments open the door wide for the Communists to pose as reformers and to press for united fronts. When we support such governments and they fall, our prestige and influence may tumble down with them.

Ataturk, who ruled Turkey for nearly a generation, was a dictator of the non-Communist left. We could not always endorse his methods. But since his government was rooted in popular support, he was able to put through vitally needed reforms, encourage the participation of his people, and lay the foundation for increasing democracy. Such a government deserves our help.

Fifth. Finally, in granting economic assistance, a country's political importance must be taken into account. This will be measured by its population, the size of its territory, its resources, its influence, and its location.

Although my purpose here today is to stress general principles and not their specific application, I may say parenthetically that the Republic of India, measured against the five standards I have listed, qualifies in special degree for sustained, expanded American economic aid.

With her 400 million people and her vast natural resources, India is not just "another underdeveloped country." It is a continent comparable in size and potential political influence to Europe.

The population of India nearly equals that of Africa and South America combined. In a single Indian state, Uttar Pradesh, there are more people than in Italy, France, or the United Kingdom.

Through its tough-minded tax system and equally tough controls on luxury imports, India has demonstrated its willingness to make major sacrifices in its own behalf.

India inherited an outstanding British-trained civil service, the most efficient in all Asia, and it has kept that service at a high degree of competence.

India has completed one five-year plan and is now half way through her second. A third, for which American, British, German, and Canadian assistance is sorely needed, is now in process of debate and discussion.

Finally, India stands today as the one political and economic alternative to China in Asia. If the Indian democratic experiment fails, whatever long-range hope may exist for freedom in the vast arc between Tokyo and Casablanca, falls with it.

On the basis of these practical considerations, I believe that India should be assured the intensive long-term investment and technical support needed to meet its economic development objectives.

Such countries as Pakistan, the Philippines, Formosa, Vietnam, Israel, Ghana, Tunisia, Chile, Costa Rica and several others could also meet the standards I have in mind.

As the capacity of still other countries approaches these criteria, and we see that more long-term aid there can be put to effective use, they should receive similar assistance from us.

Countries which are now unable to meet minimum development standards should tactfully be told that they cannot expect investment assistance from us until they have created their own internal basis for successful growth.

Most emphatically, Mr. Speaker, this does not mean that we should turn our backs on them. On the contrary, there is much that we can and should continue to do to help.

We should offer to assist them in the creation of a comprehensive economic development plan which enables them to use their own resources to the best possible advantage.

We should help provide tax experts, engineering survey teams, and other technicians to create a workable administrative base.

We should encourage them to place import controls on luxury imports purchased for their wealthy upper class so that their scarce foreign exchange can be used for the essentials needed by the people.

We should urge them to inaugurate land reforms and suggest expert advisers to help them. In Japan and Formosa American government experts took the lead in promoting a program of private land ownership that has helped the peasants in these two countries set records both for agricultural productivity and for the expansion of rural democracy.

More specifically and immediately we can help these nations to finance individual projects that are worthwhile in their own right, that are not dependent on the economy of the country as a whole, and that are clearly in the people's interest.

An example might be a modern hospital in the national capital with training facilities for doctors and nurses and an outpatient clinic system for the villages; or an expanded and improved university or agricultural experiment college.

I recognize the fact that some form of economic aid—officially called "defense support" or "special assistance"—is needed for straight political purposes, for compensatory economic reasons, to backstop military aid, or as an expedient rental fee for the use of a military base.

But I submit, Mr. Speaker, that in recent years such aid has been unduly expanded.

Mutual security implies a partnership. It can and must be a two-way street. Yet over and over again we have been pressured into giving millions to governments to pay for the use of air-bases designed to prevent their own destruction as well as ours.

American representatives abroad can and must make greater progress in placing our mutual security efforts in the military field on a true partnership basis.

Lessons from Iraq

My criticisms of the planning and administration of many of our foreign aid programs involve both military and economic assistance. Iraq provides a case in point. A brief review of developments there illustrates the need for a more realistic and less military-oriented approach.

On several occasions in 1953 and 1954 Nasser requested arms from the United States. This assistance was wisely refused, largely on the grounds that it would disrupt the balance of power with Israel, and thereby increase the danger of a clash between these neighboring nations.

However, in the spring of 1954, the Administration agreed to send military aid to Iraq, which not only threatened the destruction of Israel, but which also was in direct conflict with Egypt for the leadership of the Arab bloc.

The Egyptians protested on the ground that this assistance represented a deliberate American effort to split the Arab world, and that it ignored Egypt's interests. These protests were disregarded.

In February 1955, the Baghdad Pact was set up to add the military "weight" of Iraq, Iran, and Pakistan to that of Turkey. Its stated purpose was to deter Soviet military aggression toward the Persian Gulf.

In the spring of that year the Congress was informed that the northern tier added greatly to the security of the region from Communist invasion and that under our ally, Nuri es-Said, Iraq was the "keystone of the central arch."

However, Nuri himself declared repeatedly that the pact was directed primarily against Israel. Asked why the Western powers were supplying Iraq with such vast quantities of arms if, as he claimed, Iraq had undertaken no obligations toward the West, Nuri reportedly threw up his hands and laughed: "Who knows? Maybe they're mad."

In Cairo, other Arab leaders did not fail to recognize that the Baghdad Pact called for much more substantial American arms shipments to Iraq. After his protests over these shipments had again been rejected, Nasser announced in November that Egypt had negotiated a military agreement with the Soviet Union.

These were not the only factors in this cause-and-effect relationship, to be sure. But these events were part of a chain of events that led to Nasser's seizure of the canal and ended with the British-French-Israel attack on Egypt.

During this period, substantial American economic and technical assistance was also flowing to Iraq. Those responsible for administering this program reported to Congress that this help, together with the oil revenues available from the Iraqi government, seemed to assure Iraq's economic success.

However, little effort was made to see that the people of Iraq benefited directly from our joint efforts. Thus the new irrigation programs, while vastly increasing the income of the landlords, brought only minor gains to the cultivators.

Iraq's gross national product rose rapidly. But because luxury imports were not curbed, because progressive tax programs were not introduced, and because land reforms were postponed, the increasing income served only to expand further the already explosive gap between rich and poor.

As I wrote in a book in 1957:

> Iraq is richly endowed with oil to provide foreign exchange, with the great Tigris and Euphrates Rivers to provide irrigation water, and with ample land. Able engineers and technicians, well supplied with capital, are now working vigorously to develop these resources.
>
> But engineering miracles will not in themselves create a happy, orderly society. Most of the Iraqi land is in the hands of a relatively few politically powerful landlords.
>
> Unless there are sweeping changes in land ownership, plus rural extension programs to supply improved seeds, tools and credit, the newly created income will go largely to this fortunate minority, while the bitterness and frustration of the villages increases.

In the summer of 1958, the situation blew up and Colonel Kassim's government took power. Since then Communist influence has gained steadily and qualified observers now believe that Iraq is gradually moving into a situation where Soviet control will be inevitable.

Here, Mr. Speaker, we have an example of what happens to our interests when we overlook the political, economic and local realities in quest of a nebulous military security. In this case, as in others, we helped thereby to open the doors to the very forces which we have sought to contain.

In the streets of Baghdad, Communist-led mobs now shout insults at our representatives. American military equipment which we gave Iraq to oppose Communist aggression may ultimately be used by the Communists themselves against our friends the Israelis, our allies the Turks, or even ourselves.

I may add, Mr. Speaker, that there may be other equally calamitous case histories unless we soon bring our passion for military answers to complex political situations under better control.

The Iraq example and others raise an obvious further question. What about the effect of the standards which I have proposed on the leaders of unprepared nations whose good will is essential to us?

Will the system which I have proposed be construed and resented as political interference by nations which fail to qualify?

If we were to use our aid to pressure such nations into following our lead in the cold war, resentment would be inevitable. But is it unreasonable for the American people, who themselves pay such heavy taxes, to ask that their assistance be efficiently and honestly used?

My experience in Asia and Africa leads me to believe that the principles which I have proposed will be readily accepted, provided they are presented by tactful American negotiators, supported by a firm congressional mandate.

Indeed, I am confident that most governments can be persuaded that these criteria are essential in their own long-range interests. Many of them will welcome such standards as a lever with which to persuade reactionary elements within their own countries to cease blocking constructive reforms.

Therefore I propose that the mutual security bill should clearly outline the basis on which we intend our technical assistance and development loans to be distributed.

One Billion for Development Loan Fund

My final proposal, Mr. Speaker, involves the allocation of funds within the mutual security budget.

Although military assistance to nations which have genuine need for it must be maintained and even increased, the standards which I have suggested should result in military aid reductions in other areas.

My proposed standards for the distribution of economic aid will result in additional savings. In anticipation of such savings, and even without them, I strongly urge that the authorization for the Development Loan Fund be increased from the $700 million requested to $1 billion for fiscal year 1960.

The Development Loan Fund may well become the most creative and effective foreign policy instrument that we have organized in recent years. It is soundly conceived and is being administered with increasing competence and sensitivity.

The $700 million requested this year for the Development Loan Fund is clearly inadequate in terms of our national objectives. This figure could easily be raised to $1 billion within the present budgetary confines of the $3.9 billion mutual security request.

In my earlier remarks I have suggested how the $300 million difference could be saved from other aspects of this program. But whether this extra $300 million is derived inside or outside the program, it is clear that we can both afford it and ought to provide it.

Mr. Speaker, in offering these criticisms and observations, I would like to emphasize that I do not imply that our difficulties started with the election of 1952. On the contrary, many of the mistakes to which I refer were begun under the previous Administration of which I was a part.

There are champions of foreign aid in the Administration and the Republican party in Congress who are as anxious as any of us to place this essential program on a more solid foundation. Some of its influential and effective opponents, moreover, are to be found among my Democratic colleagues.

But regardless of party affiliations, I believe that the time has come for friends of this program to say bluntly in public what they have been saying in private, and to call on the Congress and the Administration to make the beginnings at least of a fresh start.

If the new direction and emphasis which I have proposed is accepted by the Congress, we will demonstrate to the world that our mutual security program is more than a temporary cold war gambit, and that we have embarked on a determined, long-range program designed to give men everywhere the opportunity to live under governments of their own choosing in a world of increasing prosperity and peace.

It will curb wasteful and politically disrupting shipments of American military equipment to countries which are not under direct threat from Communist aggression.

It will help establish priorities in our economic aid allocations so that those governments and people best able to use our assistance in a fruitful and beneficial way will receive the first consideration.

It will put other governments on notice that major additional help from the United States awaits their own willingness to sacrifice as others are sacrificing in terms of internal taxes, luxury import controls, land reforms, careful economic planning and personnel training.

It will also indicate that vital though we know the foreign aid program to be, the Congress does not regard it as a cure-all ointment to be applied indiscriminately to all international pains and bruises, no matter what kind or how severe.

Most important of all, Mr. Speaker, it will indicate the Congress of the United States is in a mood for changes in the basic legislation, that we are convinced that an intelligent overhaul of this program is long overdue, and that at the next session we will welcome a redirection of the present program by those responsible for its administration.

ANTI-WESTERNISM: CAUSE AND CURE [3]

VERA MICHELES DEAN [4]

This speech was delivered at the Conference of the National Association of Women Deans and Counselors in Cleveland, Ohio, on March
21, 1959. It deals succinctly and penetratingly with a major problem
underlying the struggles in many parts of the world. As editor of the
Foreign Policy Association, and director of the Non-Western Civilizations
Program at the University of Rochester, Mrs. Dean brings uncommon
experience and insight to bear upon this theme.

For an outline of Mrs. Dean's proposal for the development of a
program of non-Western civilizations in schools and colleges, readers are
invited to examine her Inglis Lecture entitled "The American Student
and the Non-Western World," published by the Harvard University Press
in 1956.

In Cuba, one of our Latin American neighbors, Fidel Castro
denounces the United States. In Iraq, until 1958 an active member of the Baghdad pact, crowds jeer at an American diplomat,
and a Communist-dominated regime comes to power. The
mayor of Manila, speaking on Edward R. Murrow's *Small
World* TV program, tells us why we are losing friends in Asia
in terms so bitter as to befit a foe rather than a friend of the
United States.

As these and other incidents are reported from around the
globe, Americans ask themselves: Why are these non-Western
peoples against the West—and particularly why are they against
the United States? What is anti-Westernism? And how can
it be cured?

So deeply is the West imbued with the sense of benefits it
has conferred on the non-Western areas in the past, and is
ready to confer in the future, that we find it difficult to believe
anti-Westernism can exist and flourish without the help of
communism. Yet, this is the harsh reality we must face in

[3] Text furnished by Mrs. Dean, with permission for this reprint.
[4] For biographical note, see Appendix.

Asia, the Middle East, and Africa if we are not to fall prey to perilous illusions.

The Russians did not need to lift a finger, fire a gun, or spend a single ruble to foment anti-Westernism in Egypt or Saudi Arabia, in Indonesia or Jordan. It's in the air. It is deeply imbedded in the consciousness of peoples who have lived under the rule of Britain, France, or the Netherlands, not of Russia. True, the Russians capitalize with marked success on a sentiment against the West which corresponds to their own, but they did not in the first place create it. This sentiment can exist and has existed apart from communism—just as some plants need no soil or fertilizer to remain alive. In fact, anti-Westernism was a sturdy plant in Russia itself during the nineteenth century under the czars, long before the Bolsheviks came on the scene.

But, if these manifestations in Russia were not initially a product of communism, were they an exclusive product of Russia's historical development? Is the anti-Westernism we see today in other areas of the world just a carbon copy of that practiced in Russia? Would it vanish if the West could discover some magic formula for eliminating Russia or sealing it off from the rest of the world?

The answer, disappointing as it is for the West, must be in the negative. From New Delhi to Cairo, from Jakarta to Karachi and Nairobi, men and women who have never read Marx, Lenin, or Stalin, and who often abhor what they know of Russia, are in the grip of the same emotions and ideas which fan the as yet unfinished controversy between Westernizers and Slavophiles in Russia. Their anti-Westernism, like that of the Russians, is an explosive mixture of contradictory reactions inspired by rising nationalism.

Non-Westerners admire our material achievements—the fruits of modern science and technology. They long to have their own peoples benefit by these fruits, to which they feel entitled by reason of living in the twentieth century; this is the essence of what has been well called the revolution of rising expectations. But they realize, with a poignancy which no

Westerner, however sympathetic, can possibly understand—because like intense fear or joy it cannot be expressed in rational terms but must be experienced to be known—that their own countries are poor and retarded, ridden with disease and ignorance. The contrast between what they see around them, in Egypt or Indonesia, and what they painfully wish to achieve is so staggering as to fill them with a sense of hopelessness and frustration. Instead of trying to escape from this state of mind by tackling the nearest practical job, no matter how modest it may be, they are likely to vent their feelings of disappointment against the West, making it the scapegoat for all the ills from which they and their countrymen suffer.

The situation becomes all the more painful—for non-Western peoples and for the West—where the rulers, today or in the recent past, are or have been Westerners who may well have concentrated on their own interests such as the building of strategic facilities or the development of resources needed by Western industry, rather than on improvement of the economic, social, and political conditions in the areas under their control. Then the anti-Westernism which is found even in independent nations such as Japan becomes dangerously aggravated by anticolonialism and, since the foreign rulers are representatives of white nations, also by racialism. To all these feelings must be added the fear of some, who want to maintain ancient political and religious customs, that the impact of the West will destroy the fabric of the nation's traditional life. They want to oust all Westerners before this horrifying prospect has come to pass.

We, however, are particularly puzzled by the tendency of the non-Western nations to denounce Western colonialism yet say little or nothing about the colonialism of the USSR. Here again Russia's past experience is much closer to that which Asia, the Middle East, and Africa are now undergoing than is the experience of the Western nations. Russia itself was a relatively backward nation as late as the 1920's. It, too, both wanted to learn from the West yet feared its impact on institutions and on national security.

This does not mean, and should not be interpreted to mean, that the Asian and African countries accept Russia without criticisms or qualms. They are aware of the dangers of eventual pressure from Moscow. They are not enthusiastic about Russian dictatorship—although, being often accustomed to authoritarianism at home, they are less repelled by it abroad than the nations of the Atlantic community, where democracy is—more or less—an old story. Russia was not invited to the Afro-Asian conference at Bandung in 1955, presumably because it is a Eurasian, not an Asian or African, country. But Russia's experience in modernizing its economy and in making the difficult transition from ancient times to the nuclear age within a third of a century is of intense interest to all non-Western areas, which feel that they have more to learn, in a practical way, from a country far closer to their current problems and experiences than from such advanced nations as the U.S.A. and Britain. This sense of affinity with Russia—economic and social if not always political—on the part of non-Western peoples of diverse religious faiths, political traditions, and international aspirations constitutes our most difficult hurdle in our efforts to find a cure for anti-Westernism.

This cure cannot be found by denouncing communism, by demanding that the non-Western nations abandon all contacts with Russia and Communist China, or by threatening to cut off aid unless they agree to join our side. Such moves would merely reinforce their hostility to and suspicion of the West and cause them to strengthen rather than weaken their still tenuous bonds with Moscow.

As in the case of some other troubles, the most promising remedy is the hair of the dog. The cure for anti-Westernism is Westernization, but it cannot be forced on peoples by military pressure or financial handouts. Nasser in Egypt or Nehru in India, like the Japanese after 1867 or the Russians after 1917, must be free to take the initiative in accepting or rejecting what the West has to offer. They must be free to pick and choose those features of our development they think best adapted to their own particular needs.

The essence of anti-Westernism, in Czarist Russia as in the USSR and other areas, is resistance to the assumption, which the West makes as a matter of course, that our civilization is superior to the civilizations of other regions and represents a norm which should be the ideal goal of Asians, Arabs, and Africans. When Glubb Pasha, upon reaching London after his expulsion from Jordan, was asked what it was the West had done wrong, he said that, while the West had committed mistakes, it had also done much good but that its main error is its "superciliousness" toward the non-West. If the West is to succeed, it must learn to restrain its natural feeling of pride in its own achievements— a feeling which, when transposed to non-Western lands, looks and sounds like arrogance—and display modesty in offering to improve the conditions of Egyptians or Indians.

We must, moreover, constantly bear in mind that, as a matter of historical fact, many of these today economically under-developed countries had achieved a high type of civilization and culture when our own ancestors were still relative savages. It is no wonder, then, that they think they have something to preserve.

Nor is it enough for us to point out that the Communist powers now practice the imperialism which the Western nations are in process of relinquishing. For Asia, Africa and the Middle East, colonialism and imperialism have been associated with the West, and symbolized by the unequal treatment accorded by whites to non-whites. What Russia does in Eastern Europe, repugnant as it may be to all non-Communists, is regarded as a conflict between white peoples. The situation changes, however, when non-whites try to subjugate and repress non-whites, as shown by the sharp reaction in Asia against Communist China's actions in Tibet.

What, then, can the United States do to counter Soviet influence? First, we must renew our efforts to facilitate orderly self-determination for those peoples who are still under colonial rule. This does not mean that all will benefit by achieving independence overnight but that we should show genuine concern for their desire to rule themselves in at least a limited form—

perhaps, for a stated period of time, under the supervision of the United Nations.

Second, when we advocate independence, we must accept the fact that independence includes the right for a free nation to choose its own course in world affairs. We must stop criticizing those of the non-Western nations which, like India or Burma, choose neutralism in preference to membership in one or other of the military blocs that have emerged out of the cold war.

Third, we must look at foreign aid not merely as a weapon in the cold war. We must understand that it is in our national interest to give aid to the underdeveloped countries, even if communism did not exist, in order to improve economic and social conditions in the world community of which we are a part. Once we realize that the goal of foreign aid is not just to defeat communism but to advance the development of non-Western areas, then we should think of long-term aid of a more substantial character than we have undertaken in the past. Economists calculate that we could and should allocate $3 billion a year during two or three decades for economic, as distinguished from military, aid. This figure may seem large, but it is less than 1 per cent of our national income.

Fourth, we must realize that foreign aid cannot be considered apart from foreign trade. The non-Western nations have no desire to become permanent pensioners. They do not just want to receive handouts; they want to stand on their own feet and gain self-respect. But they can do this only if they can repay the long-term loans we may make to them. And this they can do only if they can sell their products in Western markets. This means that we and our allies must rethink the character of world trade.

And, finally, we must learn that relations with the non-Western nations, if they are to be successful, have to be a two-way street. We have much to offer in terms of democratic procedures and technological skills, but we can greatly enrich ourselves by sharing their contributions to the world's cultural heritage through religion, philosophy, art, literature, and music.

This five-point program may sound like a tall order. But no one who has faith in the American way of life can believe that we are unable to meet Russia's challenge for peacetime competition in the non-Western World. As the *New Yorker* said about the world domination dreams of the Nazis when Germany conquered France in 1941: "We, too, can dream dreams and see visions."

THE ROLE OF THE PRESIDENT [5]

JOHN F. KENNEDY [6]

One of the first presidential aspirants to announce his availability, Senator Kennedy (Democrat, Massachusetts) carried on an energetic program of travel and speechmaking. Moreover, he dared to tackle head-on some subjects which are both delicate and politically dangerous. Such was the case on January 14, 1960, when he appeared before the National Press Club in Washington to set forth his conception of the role of the presidency during the sixties. Asserting that the American presidency in the sixties "will demand more than ringing manifestoes from the rear of the battle," Kennedy drew liberally from historical examples to contrast his analysis of President Eisenhower's interpretation of the presidency with what he thought the interpretation must be in the decade ahead. James Reston of the New York *Times* called this "the first really serious speech of the formal campaign."

The speech brought a prompt reply from Vice President Nixon. In defense of President Eisenhower's record, Nixon remarked that some Presidents got results by "table pounding" while others gave effective leadership through persuasion.

Senator Kennedy was nominated for the presidency at the Democratic Convention in July 1960.

The modern presidential campaign covers every issue in and out of the platform from cranberries to Creation. But the public is rarely alerted to a candidate's views about the central issue on which all the rest turn. That central issue—and the point of my comments this noon—is not the farm problem or defense or India. It is the presidency itself.

Of course a candidate's views on specific policies are important—but Theodore Roosevelt and William Howard Taft shared policy views with entirely different results in the White House. Of course it is important to elect a good man with good intentions—but Woodrow Wilson and Warren G. Harding were both good men of good intentions—so were Lincoln and Buchanan—but there is a Lincoln Room in the White House, and no Buchanan Room.

---

[5] Text furnished by Senator Kennedy, with permission to reprint in this volume of the Reference Shelf. Full rights over this speech are held by Senator Kennedy.

[6] For biographical note, see Appendix; for references to earlier speeches, see Cumulative Author Index.

The history of this nation—its brightest and its bleakest pages—has been written largely in terms of the different views our Presidents have had of the presidency itself. This history ought to tell us that the American people in 1960 have an imperative right to know what any man bidding for the presidency thinks about the place he is bidding for—whether he is aware of and willing to use the powerful resources of that office—whether his model will be Taft—or Roosevelt—Wilson—or Harding.

Not since the days of Woodrow Wilson has any candidate spoken on the presidency itself before the votes have been irrevocably cast. Let us hope that the 1960 campaign, in addition to discussing the familiar issues where our positions too often blur, will also talk about the presidency itself—as an instrument for dealing with those issues—as an office with varying roles, powers and limitations.

During the past eight years, we have seen one concept of the presidency at work. Our needs and hopes have been eloquently stated—but the initiative and follow-through have too often been left to others. And too often his own objectives have been lost by the President's failure to override objections from within his own party, in the Congress or even in his Cabinet.

The American people in 1952 and 1956 may well have preferred this detached, limited concept of the presidency after twenty years of fast-moving, creative presidential rule. Perhaps historians will regard this as necessarily one of those frequent periods of consolidation, a time to draw breath, to recoup our national energy. To quote the State of the Union Message: "No Congress . . . on surveying the state of the nation, has met with a more pleasing prospect than that which appears at the present time." Unfortunately this is not Mr. Eisenhower's last message to the Congress, but Calvin Coolidge's. He followed to the White House Mr. Harding, whose "sponsor" declared very frankly that the times did not demand a first-rate President. If true, the times and the man met.

But the question is what do the times—and the people demand for the next four years in the White House? They demand a vigorous proponent of the national interest—not a passive broker for conflicting private interests. They demand a man capable of acting as the Commander-in-Chief of the Grand Alliance, not merely a bookkeeper who feels that his work is done when the numbers on the balance sheet come out even. They demand that he be the head of a responsible party, not rise so far above politics as to be invisible—a man who will formulate and fight for legislative policies, not be a casual bystander to the legislative process.

Today a restricted concept of the presidency is not enough. For beneath today's surface gloss of peace and prosperity are increasingly dangerous, unsolved, long-postponed problems—problems that will inevitably explode to the surface during the next four years of the next administration—the growing missile gap, the rise of Communist China, the despair of the underdeveloped nations, the explosive situations in Berlin and in the Formosa Straits, the deterioration of NATO, the lack of an arms control agreement, and all the domestic problems of our farms, cities and schools.

This Administration has not faced up to these and other problems. Much has been said—but I am reminded of the old Chinese proverb: "There is a great deal of noise on the stairs but nobody comes into the room."

The President's State of the Union Message reminded me of the exhortation from King Lear that goes: "I will do such things . . . what they are I know not . . . but they shall be the wonders of the earth."

In the decade that lies ahead—in the challenging, revolutionary sixties—the American presidency will demand more than ringing manifestoes issued from the rear of the battle. It will demand that the President place himself in the very thick of the fight, that he care passionately about the fate of the people he leads, that he be willing to serve them at the risk of incurring their momentary displeasure.

As Chief Executive

Whatever the political affiliation of our next President, whatever his views may be on all the issues and problems that rush in upon us, he must above all be the Chief Executive in every sense of the word. He must be prepared to exercise the fullest powers of his office—all that are specified and some that are not. He must master complex problems as well as receive one-page memoranda. He must originate action as well as study groups. He must reopen the channels of communication between the world of thought and the seat of power.

Ulysses Grant considered the President "a purely administrative officer." If he administered the government departments efficiently, delegated his functions smoothly, and performed his ceremonies of state with decorum and grace, no more was to be expected of him. But that is not the place the presidency was meant to have in American life. The President is alone, at the top—the loneliest job there is, as Harry Truman has said.

If there is destructive dissension among the services, he alone can step in and straighten it out—instead of waiting for unanimity. If administrative agencies are not carrying out their mandate—if a brush-fire threatens some part of the globe—he alone can act, without waiting for the Congress. If his farm program fails, he alone deserves the blame, not his Secretary of Agriculture.

"The President is at liberty, both in law and conscience, to be as big a man as he can." So wrote Professor Woodrow Wilson. But President Woodrow Wilson discovered that to be a big man in the White House inevitably brings cries of dictatorship. So did Lincoln and Jackson and the two Roosevelts. And so may the next occupant of that office, if he is the man the times demand. But how much better it would be, in the turbulent sixties, to have a Roosevelt or a Wilson than to have another James Buchanan, cringing in the White House, afraid to move.

Nor can we afford a Chief Executive who is praised primarily for what he did not do, the disasters he prevented, the bills he vetoed—a President *wishing* his subordinates would produce more missiles or build more schools. We will need instead what the Constitution envisioned: a Chief Executive who is the vital center of action in our whole scheme of government.

As Legislative Leader

This includes the legislative process as well. The President cannot afford—for the sake of the office as well as the nation— to be another Warren G. Harding, described by one backer as a man who "would, when elected, sign whatever bill the Senate sent him—and not send bills for the Senate to pass." Rather he must know when to lead the Congress, when to consult it and when he should act alone.

Having served 14 years in the Legislative Branch, I would not look with favor upon its domination by the Executive. Under our government of "power as the rival of power," to use Hamilton's phrase, Congress must not surrender its responsibilities. But neither should it dominate. However large its share in the formulation of domestic programs, it is the President alone who must make the major decisions of our foreign policy. That is what the Constitution wisely commands. And even domestically, the President must initiate policies and devise laws to meet the needs of the nation. And he must be prepared to use all the resources of his office to ensure the enactment of that legislation—even when conflict is the result.

By the end of his term, Theodore Roosevelt was not popular in the Congress—particularly when he criticized an amendment to the Treasury appropriation which forbade the use of Secret Servicemen to investigate congressmen! And the feeling was mutual—Roosevelt saying: "I do not much admire the Senate, because it is such a helpless body when efficient work is to be done." And Woodrow Wilson was even more bitter after his frustrating quarrels—asked if he might run for the Senate in 1920, he replied: "Outside of the United States, the Senate does not amount to a damn. And inside the United States, the Senate is mostly despised. They haven't had a thought down there in fifty years."

But, however bitter their farewells, the facts of the matter are that Roosevelt and Wilson did get things done—not only through their executive powers, but through the Congress as well. Calvin Coolidge, on the other hand, departed Washington with the cheers of Congress still ringing in his ears. But when his World Court bill was under fire on Capitol Hill, he sent no messages, gave no encouragement to the bill's leaders and paid little or no attention to the whole proceeding—and the cause of world justice was set back.

To be sure, Coolidge had held the usual White House breakfasts with congressional leaders—but they were aimed, as he himself said, at "good fellowship," not a discussion of "public business." And at his press conferences, according to press historians, where he preferred to talk about the local flower show and its exhibits, reporters who finally extracted from him a single sentence—"I'm against that bill"—would rush to file tongue-in-cheek dispatches, proclaiming that: "President Coolidge, in a fighting mood, today served notice on Congress that he intended to combat, with all the resources at his command, the pending bill. . . ."

But in the coming years, we will need a *real* fighting mood in the White House—a man who will not retreat in the face of pressure from his congressional leaders—who will not let down those supporting his views on the floor. Divided government over the past six years has only been further confused by this lack of legislative leadership. To restore it next year will help restore purpose to both the presidency and the Congress.

As Party Leader

The facts of the matter are that legislative leadership is not possible without party leadership, in the most political sense—and Mr. Eisenhower prefers to stay above politics (although a weekly news magazine last fall reported the startling news, and I quote, that "President Eisenhower is emerging as a major political figure"). When asked, early in his first term, how he liked the "game of politics," he replied with a frown that his questioner was using a derogatory phrase. "Being President," he said, "is a very great experience . . . But the word 'politics' . . . I have no great liking for that."

But no President, it seems to me, can escape politics. He has not only been chosen by the nation—he has been chosen by his party. And if he insists that he is "President of all the people" and should therefore offend none of them—if he blurs the issues and differences between the parties—if he neglects the party machinery and avoids his party's leadership—then he has not only weakened the political party as an instrument of the democratic process—he has dealt a blow to the democratic process itself.

I prefer the example of Abe Lincoln, who loved politics with the passion of a born practitioner. For example, he waited up all night in 1863 to get the crucial returns on the Ohio governorship. When the Unionist candidate was elected, Lincoln wired: "Glory to God in the highest! Ohio has saved the nation!"

As a Moral Leader

But the White House is not only the center of political leadership. It must be the center of moral leadership—a "bully pulpit," as Theodore Roosevelt described it. For only the President represents the national interest. And upon him alone converge all the needs and aspirations of all parts of the country, all departments of the government, all nations of the world.

It is not enough merely to represent prevailing sentiment— to follow McKinley's practice, as described by Joe Cannon, of "keeping his ear so close to the ground he got it full of grasshoppers." We will need in the sixties a President who is willing and able to summon his national constituency to its finest hour—to alert the people to our dangers and our opportunities— to demand of them the sacrifices that will be necessary. Despite the increasing evidence of a lost national purpose and a soft national will, F.D.R.'s words in his First Inaugural still ring true: "In every dark hour of our national life, a leadership of frankness and vigor has met with that understanding and support of the people themselves which is essential to victory."

Roosevelt fulfilled the role of moral leadership. So did Wilson and Lincoln, Truman and Jackson and Teddy Roosevelt. They led the people as well as the government—they fought for great ideals as well as bills. And the time has come to demand that kind of leadership again.

And so, as this vital campaign begins, let us discuss the issues the next President will face—but let us also discuss the powers and tools with which he must face them. For he must endow that office with extraordinary strength and vision. He must act in the image of Abraham Lincoln summoning his wartime Cabinet to a meeting on the Emancipation Proclamation. That Cabinet had been carefully chosen to please and reflect many elements in the country. But "I have gathered you together," Lincoln said, "to hear what I have written down. I do not wish your advice about the main matter—that I have determined for myself."

And later, when he went to sign it after several hours of exhausting handshaking that had left his arm weak, he said to those present: "If my name goes down in history, it will be for this act. My whole soul is in it. If my hand trembles when I sign this Proclamation, all who examine the document hereafter will say: 'He hesitated.' "

But Lincoln's hand did not tremble. He did not hesitate. He did not equivocate. For he was the President of the United States.

It is in this spirit that we must go forth in the coming months and years.

PRESIDENTIAL INABILITY:
THE CONSTITUTIONAL PROBLEM [7]

GEORGE COCHRAN DOUB [8]

According to the New York *Times*, "there is nothing he [George Cochran Doub] would rather do than stand in a courtroom and argue a great case for the United States Government." On a recent occasion, October 1959, America had an opportunity to watch him carry out such an assignment in his capacity as assistant attorney general of the United States in charge of the Civil Division. He fought for the injunction under the Taft-Hartley law against the steel workers, then on strike.

Among the constitutional problems that have engaged Doub's attention is presidential inability. In the following address, he urged action on Senate Joint Resolution 40, a proposed amendment which he discussed with incisiveness and clarity. The speech was delivered at a dinner of the Federal Bar Association in honor of the Federal Judges of the Seventh Circuit, in Chicago, Illinois, on June 11, 1959.

On March 4, 1881, James A. Garfield, who as a boy drove the mule team of a canal boat on the Ohio Canal, became President of the United States. Only four months later, Garfield drove in his carriage from the White House down Pennsylvania Avenue to the Baltimore and Potomac Railroad depot on Sixth Street intending to take a train to New England. As he walked through the station arm-in-arm with Secretary of State James G. Blaine, an assassin stepped forward with a cocked revolver and fired two shots at Garfield striking him in the arm and side. When the lunatic, Charles J. Guiteau, was seized and dragged through the crowd, he cried, "Arthur is President of the United States now."

Garfield lay in a coma for eighty days completely unable to perform the duties of President. During that period, he performed only one official act—the signing of an extradition paper. The total incapacity of the President during this period, we are told, had a harmful effect on the country. Considerable

[7] Text furnished by Mr. Doub, with permission for this reprint.
[8] For biographical note, see Appendix.

government business could not be conducted nor could important officials be appointed. It has been said that the nation's foreign relations, lacking the direction of the Chief Executive, seriously deteriorated. Only routine business was handled by department heads.

Yet, nothing was done. There was criticism that Secretary of State Blaine was attempting to usurp the President's duties and there were insistent demands that Vice President Chester A. Arthur act. After sixty days, a Cabinet meeting was held in which it was unanimously voted that Vice President Arthur should assume the powers of the presidential office. But would he become President and thus preclude Garfield from returning to office? Opinions were divided. The members of the Cabinet voted 4-3, with Attorney General Wayne MacVeagh among the majority, that Arthur would become President and would thus permanently oust Garfield from office. The majority relied upon the fact that upon the three prior occasions of the death of the Chief Executive, the Vice President had become President and the language of the Constitution concerning death and inability was exactly the same.

The Cabinet resolved that, before Arthur should take this momentous step, Garfield should be consulted about the serious consequence to him which might attend Arthur's assumption of the powers of President. However, this could not be done by reason of Garfield's desperate condition. Arthur himself emphatically declined to take any steps to assume the powers of the President on the ground that he would not be a party to ousting Garfield from office. If Vice President Arthur had believed that he would exercise the powers of the presidency only for the duration of the President's disability, there would have been no reason for his failure to exercise those powers. Considerable sentiment developed at the time for clarification of the law, but after Garfield's death Arthur took office as President and the matter dropped.

If such uncertainty could occur during the peaceful days of 1881, how frightening would be the prospect of similar uncertainty at a time when it is essential that the nation have such continuity of official leadership as to enable critical decisions to be met and made.

In periods of peace and quiet of the past, this issue may not have been of vital importance but in the dangerous critical days of world leadership, of nuclear weapons, of the touch of the ICBM on the nerve of danger, of a powerful threatening enemy, the problem becomes one of paramount consequence. In times of almost continuous international crisis requiring immediate decisions by the Executive to safeguard the nation's interests, our future safety could possibly depend upon our ability to have provided clear definitive answers to this constitutional question.

In the event of the inability of the President to discharge the powers and duties of his office, does the Vice President succeed permanently to the presidency? Or does he act as a temporary pinch-hitter during the disability period? Who is authorized to say a President is unable to discharge his duties?

You will recall that Paragraph 6 of Section 1 of Article 11 of the Constitution provides that "in case of the removal, death, resignation and inability to discharge the powers and duties of the office of President, the same *shall* devolve on the Vice President." You will notice that the language is mandatory. "The same *shall*," not "*may*," devolve on the Vice President. "Devolve means to pass down, descend, to transfer, and the mandatory transfer to the Vice President occurs in the same way in each of the four situations: removal, death, resignation, or inability to discharge the powers and duties of the office of President. No distinction is made as to what happens in case of presidential inability and the President's removal, death, or resignation.

The Constitution states, "the same shall devolve on the Vice President. . . ." To what do the words "the same" refer? What is it that shall "devolve" upon the Vice President? Is it the *office* of the President? In that case, the President would thenceforth be permanently excluded from his office; or do only the *powers and duties* devolve upon the Vice President and in that case, his tenure as the acting chief executive would end upon the recovery of the President.

It appears that there was a constitutional question, when the issue first arose, whether the Vice President, in the case of the death of the President, became President or acting President for the balance of the term, but this doubt has now been settled by established practice.

The question first was presented when President William Henry Harrison died of pneumonia in office in 1841, one month after his inauguration, "worn away and destroyed by the hordes of applicants for public office." Did Vice President John Tyler become President or acting President? Many objected at the time to Tyler becoming President because it was believed that the precedent would establish that the same result must occur when the President became disabled. It was argued that the records of the Constitutional Convention indicated that the Convention had not intended that the Vice President become President under the succession clause but merely that he should exercise the powers and duties of the disabled President until his inability was removed. Daniel Webster, then Secretary of State, was the only Whig who was not greatly alarmed over what the Democrat, Tyler, would do in opposition to Whig policies and interests. Webster took the position that Vice President Tyler actually became President. It was Tyler's initial belief that he would act as President during Harrison's unexpired term, but reflection changed his attitude and in his "inaugural address" he boldly proclaimed that he had been called to "the high office of this confederacy."

The first paper submitted to Tyler for his signature had below the space for his signature the words "Acting President." Tyler was incensed and by a stroke of his pen eliminated the word "Acting" and signed as President, and President he became. After him, six other Vice Presidents, Fillmore, Johnson, Arthur, Theodore Roosevelt, Coolidge and Truman, did likewise upon the death of the President in office. From these precedents, it is now assumed that, in the case of the death of a President, the Vice President becomes President for the unexpired term. Yet, the very way the original doubt was resolved by these precedents has contributed to the problem in the case of the inability of the President to discharge the powers and duties of his office.

When we examine the original articles agreed upon in substance by the Constitutional Convention before their revision by the Committee of Style, we find that they made clear that upon the inability of the President to discharge the powers and duties of his office, the Vice President should exercise those powers and duties "until the inability of the President be removed."

In other words, the framers of the Constitution intended that the Vice President would be acting as President, but would not become the President. Although acting as President, he would remain in the office of Vice President.

The obscurity developed by reason of the revision made by the Committee of Style, which boiled the provision down to the simplified statement that in case of removal, death, resignation or inability to discharge the powers and duties of the office, "the same shall devolve on the Vice President."

This interpretation is borne out by the debates in the Convention indicating that the vice presidency was originally created to provide for an alternate chief executive who might function from time to time should the President be unable to exercise the powers and duties of his office. Indeed, only after the Convention decided upon this standby position did the Convention consider giving the Vice President something to do while he waited in the wings. The idea of assigning him the duty of presiding over the Senate seems to have been an afterthought.

In 1919, President Woodrow Wilson suffered a stroke while leading his great fight for the adoption of the Covenant of the League of Nations. At that time the position of the United States had developed into one of world leadership. After our spectacular military and economic exertions in World War I, and at the moment that the leader of democracy was stricken, in the midst of the postwar effort to establish a lasting peace, a dramatic Senate battle over ratification of the Versailles Treaty and of the Covenant of the League of Nations was being waged.

The illness of Wilson continued from his collapse on September 25, 1919, until the end of his presidential term on March 4, 1921. During this period of one year and five months, the President was unable to attend any Cabinet meetings or to perform most of his duties. The exact extent of his inability is not clear because his condition was carefully shielded from the public by Mrs. Wilson, his personal physician and his entourage in the White House. Indeed, even the Vice President and the Cabinet were kept in the dark about Wilson's condition. It is said that for a considerable period of time—although the precise time is subject to speculation—he was completely unable to perform *any* of the duties of his high office. It has been believed that Mrs. Wilson and the President's physician played a major role in making and deciding matters of large public policy. In any event, the administration of the Government almost was at a standstill for one and a half years.

Without the direction of the President or Vice President, Secretary of State Lansing called twenty-one Cabinet meetings in an attempt to prevent the affairs of the Government from becoming paralyzed. When Wilson heard of these meetings he accused Lansing of usurping presidential power and forced this outstanding Secretary of State to resign. Upon Lansing's suggestion that the Cabinet request Vice President Marshall to act as President, Joseph P. Tumulty, Wilson's secretary, replied: "You may rest assured that while Wilson is lying in the White House in the broad of his back I will not be a party to ousting him." At that time widespread discussion again ensued for clarification of the law, but when Wilson's term expired the matter died down again.

Now why did Wilson's personal advisers fear knowledge of his disability becoming known? I believe that there can be no doubt that a primary reason was because of their fear that public opinion would demand that Vice President Marshall take over the powers of the presidency and, if Wilson should recover, he might face a constitutional fight to regain his office.

In other words, the dangerous uncertainty of this constitutional provision was responsible for this deplorable situation. Attempts made to induce Vice President Marshall to act as President failed. The major reason Marshall was unwilling to act was because of the fear that once he did so, Wilson would be ousted permanently from the presidency.

The pernicious consequences of the belief that a Vice President actually succeeds to the presidency for the balance of the presidential term, when called upon to exercise the powers and duties of a disabled President, have been in both the Garfield and the Wilson case to frustrate the intent of the drafters of the Constitution that the nation should have an alternate chief executive ready to provide continuous executive leadership. If it had been perfectly clear that constitutionally the President could resume his powers at any time his disability ended and he was relinquishing the reins only temporarily, this dangerous problem should not have arisen in either the Garfield or Wilson administrations.

Immediately upon President Eisenhower's recovery from his heart attack in Colorado in September, 1955, he directed the Department of Justice to institute a full legal study of the constitutional problem with respect to presidential inability. His purpose was the preparation of a plan for the protection of the nation in the event any President in the future were to become disabled. After an extensive study of the problem by Attorney General Herbert Brownell, the President reviewed alternative plans and authorized the Attorney General to consult persons outside the Government for their views and criticisms. The President also sought the opinions of the members of the Cabinet at a Cabinet meeting. Finally a definitive plan proposing a constitutional amendment was prepared by Attorney General Brownell, approved by the President, orally presented by the President at a meeting of congressional leaders of both parties and publicly announced in the testimony of the Attorney General before a subcommittee of the Judiciary Committee in the House of Representatives.

President Eisenhower was the first President of the United States who had the courage, the interest and the appreciation of the problem to attempt to correct this serious deficiency of the Constitution. Every prior President shrank from attempting to deal with this delicate matter or manifested no realization of the difficulty.

On March 3, 1958, the President and the Vice President took an historic step in consultation with Attorney General William P. Rogers when they reduced to memorandum form, and published, their own understanding of the constitutional role of the Vice President as acting President during the disability of the President. The Eisenhower-Nixon understanding was stated in these terms:

The President and the Vice President have agreed that the following procedures are in accord with the purposes and provisions of Article 2, Section 1, of the Constitution, dealing with presidential inability. They believe that these procedures, which are intended to apply to themselves only, are in no sense outside or contrary to the Constitution but are consistent with its present provisions and implement its clear intent.

1. In the event of inability the President would—if possible—so inform the Vice President, and the Vice President would serve as Acting President, exercising the powers and duties of the office until the inability had ended.

2. In the event of an inability which would prevent the President from communicating with the Vice President, the Vice President, after such consultation as seems to him appropriate under the circumstances, would decide upon the devolution of the powers and duties of the office and would serve as Acting President until the inability had ended.

3. The President, in either event, would determine when the inability had ended and at that time would resume the full exercise of the powers and duties of the office.

I have no doubt that this unprecedented document, although not binding upon future Presidents and Vice Presidents, will become recognized as a notable state paper of our constitutional history.

On the day following the Eisenhower-Nixon announcement a bipartisan majority of the members of the Senate Judiciary Committee, including Senators Kefauver, Dirksen, Hruska, Hennings, Johnston, Langer, Watkins, Jenner and Butler, joined in sponsoring a proposed constitutional amendment on presidential inability which adopted the Administration's proposal with certain changes in Section 4 acceptable to the Executive. This proposed bipartisan amendment was promptly introduced in the Congress.

Section 1 restates existing law in case of the removal, death or resignation of the President.

Section 2 provides that, if a President declares in writing that he is unable to discharge the powers and duties of his office, those powers and duties shall be discharged by the Vice President as Acting President. This section assures a President in announcing his own inability that his powers and duties will be restored to him upon his recovery.

Section 3 deals with a situation in which the President is unable or unwilling to declare his own disability. In that case, the Vice President with the approval of the majority of the heads of the Executive Departments in office—that is to say, the President's Cabinet—shall make this decision. Many scholars agree that the Vice President alone now has the authority under the Constitution to make this determination. Section 3 requires the written concurrence of a majority of the members of the Cabinet.

Section 4 provides that, whenever the President declares in writing that his disability is terminated, he shall resume the exercise of the powers and duties of his office. This provision affords a constitutional guarantee to a President that he will regain the powers of his office when his disability has been removed.

The realities of the situation suggest that it is unlikely a Vice President would attempt to assume the duties of the presidency unless it were clear beyond challenge that the President was, in fact, unable to exercise the responsibilities of the office. The proposed constitutional provision proclaiming plainly that the Vice President will merely discharge the powers and duties of the presidential office for the temporary period of disability should negative any motive of usurpation. At the same time, the Vice President should not in the future under the amendment refuse—as Vice President Arthur and Vice President Marshall—to perform his constitutional duty of serving as the alternate executive temporarily when the circumstances require that he do so.

Section 4 will allow the President to resume the functions of his office although there might be a difference of opinion between the President and the Vice President whether the disability has ended. However, in the event of a dispute between them as to this, provision is made for immediate action by the Congress, whether then in session or not, to resolve the issue if raised in writing by the Vice President with the support of the majority of the Cabinet. A two-thirds vote of the members present in both Houses would be required to establish the continued existence of the President's inability. Thereafter, the announcement by the Acting President that the President's inability has ended or a resolution adopted by a majority of both Houses will restore the powers of the office to the President upon his recovery.

Historically this problem has never been one of a too aggressive Vice President but rather of a reluctant Vice President, who hesitated to exercise the powers of the President under the present succession clause of the Constitution because of the uncertainty that his action might result in the permanent elimination of the President from his office.

The essential solution is a clarifying amendment establishing that the Vice President's tenure of the presidential powers is only temporary. This provision is the foundation of the Administration's proposal submitted in 1957, resubmitted in 1958, and the bipartisan amendment proposed in the same year. The proposal implements the original understanding of the members of the Constitutional Convention as indicated in the debates and in the original articles.

There is now presented the best opportunity in our history for the solution of this problem. The time required for the ratification of a constitutional amendment will undoubtedly extend beyond the term of this Administration and accordingly will be inapplicable to it.   We do not know the person or the party that will occupy the White House in 1961, but we do know that under the Constitution, it will not be President Eisenhower.   At this moment in history, the proposed measure can be considered entirely upon its merits without any consideration of personalities or parties.

At the time of each illness of President Eisenhower, as in the case of President Garfield and President Wilson, there was a general recognition of the seriousness of this constitutional problem of succession and clamor by political leaders of both parties and the press that constructive measures be taken for its resolution.   Although the problem arises from a permanent inherent defect in our constitutional system, proposals for its resolution now lie dormant in the Congress under the press of far less significant matters.   The bipartisan constitutional amendment was proposed over a year ago yet the Senate Judiciary Committee and the House Judiciary Committee have taken no action of any kind.

An informed and responsible public opinion appears needed to secure the action which the interests of the nation plainly require.

LABOR'S POSITION ON LABOR-MANAGEMENT
REFORM LEGISLATION [9]

GEORGE MEANY [10]

The Select Senate Committee on Improper Activities in the Labor or Management Fields began its investigations in early 1957. Its revelations of the misuse of funds, extortion, unfair transactions, and other abuses resulted in various proposals for reform. Extended congressional debate ensued which eventually led to passage in the Senate of a bill sponsored by Senator John F. Kennedy and in the House of the Landrum-Griffin bill. Senator Kennedy was the chairman of the Senate-House conference that fashioned a compromise bill. It passed both houses overwhelmingly. On September 14, President Eisenhower signed the bill, known as the Labor-Management Reporting and Disclosure Act of 1959.

The proponents of "reform" legislation and the officers of AFL-CIO were of one mind in condemning corruption and undesirable elements in labor and management. The disagreements grew out of the crucial inquiry into means: How can the reforms be brought about without imposing restrictive measures upon the labor movement, without harassing the legitimate and decent unions?

President Eisenhower appealed to the nation over radio and television on August 6 for the adoption of reform legislation that would "protect the American people from the gangsters, racketeers, and other corrupt elements who have invaded the labor-management field." He asserted that the American people were not interested in the "weak" or "strong" labels currently applied to the several proposed bills. "They are interested in a law which will eliminate the abuses." He endorsed the Landrum-Griffin proposal as "a good start toward a real labor reform bill."

Following this speech, the radio listeners were able to hear George Meany, president of the AFL-CIO, give a reply—although his recorded talk had evidently been arranged before President Eisenhower announced his speaking plan.

Meany's speech dealt largely with two themes: What has the AFL-CIO done to cope with corruption in the trade union movement? What is the attitude of the AFL-CIO toward the pending reform bills? Meany favored the Shelley bill, which he described as "anti-racketeer, [but] not anti-labor."

[9] Text furnished by Albert J. Zack, Director of Department of Public Relations, AFL-CIO, with permission for this reprint.

[10] For biographical note, see Appendix; for references to earlier speeches, see Cumulative Author Index.

This is a critical moment in the legislative history of American labor. Congress is in the process of enacting what is described as labor reform legislation. The Senate already has passed a bill on this subject which the trade union movement considers detrimental to the future of American labor. Now the House of Representatives is about to consider several bills on this subject namely, the Elliott Bill, reported by the House Committee on Education and Labor—the Landrum-Griffin Bill which has the support of a coalition of Republican and southern Democratic members and the Shelley bill which has the support of the AFL-CIO.

Whatever legislation is finally enacted on this subject will undoubtedly affect labor-management relations for years to come. Beyond that, if the final measure enacted places the trade union movement in the legalistic strait jacket that some of labor's enemies so ardently desire, there is a grave possibility that the nation's economy might be adversely affected.

Let me say as emphatically as I can that the AFL-CIO is in complete accord with the great majority of the American people in favor of legislation that will help get the crooks without harassing and impeding the forward progress of legitimate and decent labor unions.

Unfortunately, there are forces at work whose only real purpose is to hamper and, if possible, to destroy the effectiveness of legitimate trade unions. They consider the exposure of corrupt leadership in a small minority of unions as too good an opportunity to be missed in order to fasten restrictive legislation on the entire movement.

Under the guise of legislation against corruption, they want to tie up legitimate union activities with legal knots—thus making it difficult, if not impossible, for the trade union movement to carry on its work for economic and social progress.

As part of their antilabor strategy these people are deliberately circulating rumors to the effect that labor is not really opposed to this bill or that bill or that labor wants no legislation at all or that labor as represented by the AFL-CIO is not really concerned with the problem of corruption.

These rumors are all false and can be proved by a quick look at the record of the AFL-CIO on this subject.

On February 9, 1955, almost five years ago, the American Federation of Labor and the Congress of Industrial Organizations reached agreement on a set of principles under which the two national trade union centers would merge into one organization. Among the principles adopted was the following, and I quote: "The merged Federation shall constitutionally affirm its determination to protect the American trade union movement from any and all corrupt influences."

On December 5, 1955, the AFL-CIO at its first convention, wrote this principle into its Constitution and provided the means for its implementation.

In the summer of 1956, many months before the McClellan Committee came into existence, the AFL-CIO proposed to the platform committees of both major party conventions that they pledge their party to the enactment of public reporting and disclosure laws to guard against abuses and corruption in the administration of health and welfare funds held in trust for the benefit of union members. Such a law has since been enacted.

Less than a year later, following the early hearings of the McClellan Committee, the AFL-CIO urged extension of the same legal safeguards for all union funds. We testified before the House and Senate Labor Committees in favor of the enactment of legislation—strong and enforceable legislation—to prevent union officials from stealing the dues money of their members or committing other flagrant abuses.

In 1957, through the authority and directives contained in the AFL-CIO Constitution, the Executive Council drew up a comprehensive set of Codes and Ethical Practices for trade unions and trade union officials and presented them to our convention in December 1957, where they were made part of the basic law of the Federation.

Was the AFL-CIO content with mere statements and constitutional declarations against corruption in the labor movement? Or did it take action to give life and meaning to its declared principles on this subject? The answer to these questions is crystal clear.

At the same convention of December 1957, at which it adopted its Ethical Practices Codes, the AFL-CIO upon the recommendation of its Executive Council, and under its democratic procedure, expelled three of its unions as being under corrupt control. This was accomplished by more than the two-thirds roll-call vote required by the Constitution. Among the unions expelled was the International Brotherhood of Teamsters, the largest union in the Federation. The combined membership of the three unions expelled represented more than 10 per cent of our entire membership.

Shortly thereafter, in March of 1958, the AFL-CIO recognized that there was still a problem to be met—the problem of protecting the membership of expelled unions as well as protecting the general public from the consequences of corrupt practices on the part of those unions.

At this juncture, the AFL-CIO publicly advocated the passage of labor reform legislation by Congress—legislation to protect the funds of union members—legislation to safeguard the rights of union members—legislation to help the government get rid of crooks operating in the labor-management field.

This was a truly significant action. Here was a group of private citizens saying to government: We will assist you in writing legislation to regulate and govern certain of our actions. Where else in American life is there a parallel? What business organization has ever done such a thing? And the record shows incidentally that business is not immune to sin nor free of racketeering elements.

The AFL-CIO at that time made one reservation: that we would not support or accept any legislation, under the guise of reform legislation, that would restrict and punish honest trade unions. That reservation still stands.

Let us see how the pending bills measure up to this test.

The Elliott Bill contains provisions that safeguard the funds of union members, that protect union members against abuses and that provide criminal penalties for a variety of intolerable racketeering practices. We are 100 per cent in favor of these provisions.

But the Elliott Bill also contains other provisions. It would place the officers of 65,000 local unions in jeopardy of being found in violation of a Federal criminal statute in discharging their normal duties. It would prohibit honorable organizational practices and procedures upon which labor has built its present-day structure. It would expose unions to the danger of endless litigation not over real issues but at the whim of one or two individuals, who might be subsidized by hostile employers or by Communists to undertake such harassment. It would make it extremely difficult for the average union to conduct its normal business in a straightforward, effective way. Because of these provisions, we must oppose and we do oppose the Elliott Bill.

Now let's see how the Landrum-Griffin Bill measures up. It also contains a number of antiracketeering provisions which are similar to those in the Elliott Bill. Again the AFL-CIO is 100 per cent in favor.

But the Landrum-Griffin Bill goes a lot further than the Elliott Bill in penalizing legitimate practices of legitimate unions. It would subject a union presiding officer to a two-year jail sentence merely for blocking a disorderly person from disrupting a meeting. It would require even the smallest local unions, without paid officers, to file a burdensome amount of red-tape reports. It would force union members against their will and against their basic principles to handle "struck" goods. It would prohibit any union from advertising to the public that an employer is unfair to labor, pays sub-standard wages or operates a sweatshop, despite Supreme Court decisions that have held a union has not only a right but a duty to speak out against such abuses. It would make it virtually impossible for the average, decent union to function effectively.

For these reasons the AFL-CIO strongly opposes the Landrum-Griffin bill.

Finally, we come to the Shelley Bill. It contains provisions against thievery and racketeering which are even stronger than those in the Elliott Bill or the Landrum-Griffin Bill.

Unlike those bills, the Shelley Bill would also require full reporting from business firms of expenditures of union-busting activities and the hiring of labor spies.

But it does not contain any provisions which would restrict, harass or punish the legitimate activities of honest and decent unions. In other words, the Shelley Bill is aimed at getting rid of crooks, instead of getting rid of unions. For those reasons we support it fully and we hope that the House of Representatives will adopt it.

We in the AFL-CIO recognize that the worst enemies of labor are those few crooked union officials who have betrayed their trust and sold out their members and made alliances with the underworld.

Because of the excesses they have committed and gotten away with, pressure has been built up for legislation that would victimize all unions, the great majority of good ones along with the few that have been corrupted.

Basically, the cure for this problem is better law enforcement. If the present laws on the statute books of our states against theft, corruption and racketeering had been properly enforced, there would be no need for new Federal law.

One thing is certain—new legislation should be aimed at the crooks, not at the decent, law-abiding unions and their decent, law-abiding members.

The Elliott Bill fails to meet this test. It places unfair burdens on legitimate unions. The Landrum-Griffin bill is much worse. It is a blunderbuss that would inflict grievous harm on all unions. It is supported by the very elements in Congress which have consistently through the years voted for the program of big business and against every progressive measure that would benefit all the American people.

That leaves the Shelley Bill. We sincerely believe it will do the job of getting rid of the crooks who have wormed their way into a few unions. We believe it will do an effective job of preventing unholy alliances between dishonest unions and dishonest employers. We are convinced that it will not interfere unnecessarily in legitimate labor-management activities. The Shelley Bill is antiracketeer, not antilabor.

These are the objectives that the AFL-CIO seeks in labor reform legislation. We urge Congress to keep its sights on these objectives. If you want to stop corruption and not harm legitimate unions, we hope you will let your congressman know immediately that you favor the Shelley Bill.

EDUCATION—FOR WHAT? [11]

FRANCIS H. HORN [12]

The American educational system continues to receive extensive analysis and evaluation. Faced by larger enrollments, a shortage of teachers, a lack of physical facilities, and rising costs of operation, the public is asking hard questions about the nature of our training programs. Moreover, it is growing impatient with wordy answers. The citizen wants assurance that youth is getting the kind and quality of training urgently needed in this troubled time. What are the goals, the objectives, toward which our education is directed?

Dr. Francis H. Horn, president of the University of Rhode Island, gives a perceptive reply to this inquiry in a speech delivered in New York City on March 25, 1960. This was the keynote address at the thirty-fifth annual spring conference of the Eastern States Association of Professional Schools for Teachers.

The most important task in the world today is education. Education is the one best hope for a world which stands at a crossroads where mankind has never stood before. One way leads toward the brightest future man has ever known—a world truly at peace, where the age-old scourges of hunger and disease, poverty and ignorance, exist no longer, where all men everywhere can know the standard of material comfort which most Americans enjoy today, where kindness, justice, and wisdom govern the affairs of men, and where each individual has the opportunity to fulfill himself to the utmost of his abilities. The other way leads toward catastrophe for all mankind; it is the road of nuclear warfare, and while its outcome cannot be surely known, the end of civilization, even the annihilation of mankind, is possible.

Reliance on military hardware is no permanent solution to this most crucial problem the world has ever faced. But a permanent solution must eventually be found. The world cannot stand forever in doubt at the crossroads; it cannot indefinitely

---

[11] Text furnished by Dr. Horn. Reprinted by permission of Dr. Horn and the *Teachers College Record.*

[12] For biographical note. see Appendix.

continue to exist perched precariously on the brink of the abyss of nuclear war. The solution must be found in education, in the work of the schools and colleges in this country and in all countries.

This means that in all nations, more and more attention must be paid to extending the benefits and improving the quality of education. It means also that more and more consideration must be given to the goals of education. If education holds the key to the future, if the work of schools and colleges is so crucially important to the welfare of the world and the individuals who make it up, what conclusions can we draw about the kind of an education we must provide our children and youth to prepare them for the years ahead? In short—education for what?

If I had only one answer to the question, I should say, "Education for tomorrow's world." In issuing the call for the Sixth White House Conference on Children and Youth, President Eisenhower stated: "The rapidly changing times in which we live, and the increasingly fast pace of change, make it incumbent upon us to do everything we can to plan ahead and to see that we prepare today's children for tomorrow's world. . . ." In view of the speed and the nature of the changes the world is likely to experience in the future, it will be difficult to do this. We cannot know for sure what the world of tomorrow will be like. What exploration of outer space will produce, for example, is still a matter of speculation.

Certainly there can be no doubt of the extent of the developments that lie ahead. The world in the past half century has made as much scientific progress as in all previous history. And yet these advances are only a beginning. Writing five years ago on "The Fabulous Future," General David Sarnoff of RCA stated that there will be such great technological progress in the next quarter century that the remarkable advances that have occurred up to the present will be "from the vantage point of 1980, a fumbling prelude." We are still only on the threshold of scientific and technological progress.

One result is the terrific increase in the world's knowledge. In the natural sciences alone, knowledge is doubling every ten years. Ten years after students graduate from college, they will have to learn things which they never heard of before, nor their professors either. This learning of new things will apply to what men do as well as to what they know. It is impossible to foresee the specific jobs that will be needed for the future and to prepare for them. Many of the jobs our fathers held are obsolete. A generation hence, many of those we hold today will have disappeared. A recent study of two industrial communities in Connecticut shows that 58 per cent of the people earn their livelihood at jobs which were non-existent fifty years ago. I suspect that because of more rapid technological change, the same situation will prevail not fifty years hence, but only twenty-five years from now.

Although the uncertainties about the future outweigh the certainties, we can be pretty sure about some developments. The life span will continue to be extended as medical science makes further advances. Recently at the National Health Forum of the National Health Council, an expert predicted that man's life would be extended, not just to the century mark, but to 140 to 150 years. Most assuredly, people will live much longer, and in better health in the later years, than ever before.

Another certainty—these "certainties" assume that the world does not blow itself to bits, but moves, however haltingly, down the road to the bright future that does lie ahead if man can learn to live with his fellow man in amity and peace—is that there will be greater leisure for all. A workweek of twenty-four or twenty-five hours will become normal for most people. One's job will no longer be what gives most meaning to one's life. One's leisure-time activities, if one becomes truly educated, will provide the more significant aspects of one's existence.

Another development of which there is no doubt is the population explosion. The demographers are constantly revising their figures on world population upward. There is little question now that the present two billion people on this planet will become six billion by the year 2000.

The population explosion suggests another certainty of which few Americans are aware. The world of tomorrow for which teachers and parents must prepare their children will not be a western world at all, but an eastern world. In the year 2000, India will have a billion people, China nearly one and two-thirds billion. The peoples of Africa also are awakening and advancing, and their population will be increasing rapidly. In the world of tomorrow the Asians and the Africans will be in the vast majority; they may indeed, as they adopt Western technology, dominate the world.

Hopefully, however, in the world of tomorrow, there will not be any dominant power or group of powers. In tomorrow's world the power structure that has prevailed since recorded history may well be obsolete. Certainly science has shrunk the world enormously. Planes will eventually circumnavigate the globe in a matter of a few hours. It will depend primarily upon education as to whether this shrunken world actually becomes the one world without which the bright future I have held out for mankind is impossible.

I have suggested enough of the more certain characteristics of the world for which schools and colleges must prepare their students. Let me now suggest some of the goals of education that we must set for the children and youth whom it will be our privilege to teach.

It should be obvious that education for a changing world will need to be directed toward certain general objectives rather than specifics—and this in spite of the fact that the world requires a greater degree of specialization than ever before. One of the goals of education should be the acceptance of change and uncertainty as necessary conditions of life. We should stop trying to counteract such acceptance. We fuss about family mobility. At present, one out of three families moves every two years. A child psychologist, speaking recently in our area, deplored the difficulty of new families attaining status in a neighborhood. "Their children," he said, "have no strong attachments to either locality or kinship groups. Such mobility increases the problem of emotional stability." But education for tomorrow's world should teach us to accept mobility, not to worry about the traditional status in a community, and not to expect it. In tomorrow's world, there will be far more mobility and more families will find themselves moving, not just to other parts of America, but to out-of-the-way places in the world. Indeed, some of us may have to set up housekeeping on the moon!

If my contention here is right—and I realize that most teachers and psychologists may think it is not—then another current emphasis must be abandoned—the emphasis on "belonging." The Fifth White House Conference on Children and Youth had as its second pledge to children: "We will help you to strengthen your sense of belonging." We have had enough of this "togetherness." The emphasis upon it, of course, does lead to problems of emotional instability when it isn't there. But we should bring up children not to want to "belong," not to lean on others, even on the members of their own family. What we should educate for is independence—independence of thought, of action, of character. In Rhode Island atop the State House is a statue of independent man. This should be the ideal of twentieth-century man even more than of the man of the seventeenth or eighteenth century, who established in Rhode Island the tradition of independence. Even as life becomes more dominated by groups, it is imperative that we develop the individual to enable him to stand on his own two feet, with or without status in a peer group or in a community.

Actually, the old concept of a community is an anachronism in the modern world. If we are to develop a sense of "belonging to the community," a phrase much used by educators, it should be directed to establishing an attitude of belonging to the world community. The child and youth of today being prepared for tomorrow's world should be taught above all to consider himself primarily as a member of the human race, to recognize that every man is his brother, that his neighbor is not the man next door, but man everywhere, regardless of the color of his skin, his ethnic background, his religious convictions, or, indeed, the nature of his cooking or his plumbing. Our children and young people should be educated for acceptance of the concept of the fatherhood of God and the brotherhood of man; they should work for the attainment of the ideal expressed in the old Chinese saying, "Under heaven there is one family; within the four seas, all men are brothers."

I have suggested thus far that the over-all answer to the question "Education for what?" is "Education for tomorrow's world." And that since tomorrow's world is one of rapid and profound change, our schools and colleges must endeavor to educate our students at all ages for accepting change, for adjusting to it.

Let me point out, however, that though I have advocated educating for adjustment to change, I am not endorsing what has been called "life adjustment" education. I deplore the whole concept. Adjusting to life should not be an over-all goal of education. The purpose of education is not to teach individuals to accept life as they find it; it is quite the opposite. Education should teach individuals to modify life—to improve the environment, to change the social ills which man is heir to, to mold the conditions of existence closer to the heart's desire. Education should make individuals want to bring about change; not just for the sake of change, but for the improvement of individual and group living.

There will be in the future many changes over which individuals have little control—the shrinking of the globe, automation, greater leisure. These should not be resisted, unless they bring evil consequences. Such changes man must be prepared to accept. He must learn to adjust without frustration and heartache. Perhaps a better word would be "adapt." If we are adequately to educate our children and young people for tomorrow's world, we must teach them to be adaptable.

In the light of what I have said about educating for change, there are two implications for teachers which are extremely important. If change is so rapid and so pervasive, if knowledge is expanding so explosively, it is evident (1) that the specific content of schooling is not so important as the habits of learning which the student acquires; and (2) that learning is a lifelong process.

It can no longer be said that even the basic tool subjects, the three R's, are unchanging. Modern mathematics has rendered a good deal of what used to be taught obsolete. In other fields, new discoveries, analyses, and interpretations may make out of date what has long been taught in literature, history, or the sciences. It becomes increasingly important, therefore, for teachers to teach students broadly, to help them to understand basic principles and to learn how to tackle problems, and, above all, to inspire them to pursue learning. If the foundation for learning is well laid, then the probability of a lifetime of learning is more certain. Such learning is imperative if the potential better world for us all is to be attained.

There is one corollary to this which must be emphasized. The problems facing mankind are greater than man has ever faced before. Never in the past has he been confronted by the possibility of his own annihilation. Conversely, never before has he had within his grasp the possibility of the good life for all. Whether or not he survives and attains the better world that is within his grasp, will, as I have said, depend primarily upon education. The solutions to the critical problems the world is facing — economic, social, political, ideological — depend upon bringing greater wisdom into the affairs of men and of nations. In the modern world, democratic or struggling to be democratic in its political systems, such wisdom must be not only at the top among the leaders, it must permeate the whole of society. Consequently, more and better education for more of the world's population is imperative. I cannot agree with critics of education today who find the solution to the world's problems in the better education of an intellectual elite. I do agree that we are tolerating a great waste of our most important resource, brainpower, in our failure to provide college and graduate education for all our ablest young people. Every effort must be made to educate all of these superior students to their maximum. But I am equally convinced that the world today requires the education of all our population to the maximum of their ability. If we are not to provide some form of higher education for *all* American youth, at least our goal must be to provide it for an increasingly large majority of American youth. And what is necessary in the United States to maintain our free society is likewise necessary elsewhere in the world if a free society is to be built and maintained there.

Since I have moved from a discussion of education in general to that of higher education, let me consider some answers to the question "Education—for What?" that are especially relevant for higher education. I wish to consider certain values which I believe will inhere in the best education regardless of the vast changes that are occurring in the world. These values are objectives of higher education for the individual. To a lesser degree, of course, they are the objectives of education at all levels. Their formation, in any case, is laid in the elementary and secondary schools. These values do not and will not change.

It should be emphasized that, while the values themselves endure essentially without regard to time or place or level of development, at least within the framework of what we call Western civilization, the means of inculcating these values, of attaining these objectives, may certainly change. In fact college and university administrations and faculties must guard against a tendency to cling to traditional but outmoded policies, programs, and practices when an evolving world requires their modification.

What are these enduring values which colleges and universities must preserve and foster? The values are intellectual and cultural, moral and spiritual—but they are not essentially vocational values. Preparation for specific vocations is an essential and important part of the task of every university. Those who decry vocationalism in higher education do the colleges and universities a great disservice and are blind to the realities of the present-day world. Never before was specialized training for specific occupations so important. But these practical studies must be joined to liberal studies in a broad and integrated curriculum. The teaching of the practical studies, moreover, must always be infused with the liberal spirit. When so taught, such studies may help to develop the qualities of mind and spirit which are the earmarks of the educated man, but vocational studies alone, however well taught, cannot produce those humane values which endure regardless of the nature of our society and the extent of our technological development.

The first and most important objective of higher education, so far as the individual is concerned, is to educate the student to think—to think for himself. No thinking machine can long be a substitute for man thinking. Automation will never supplant the human brain and make it obsolete; the future, in fact, will make even greater demands on man's mental powers. Colleges must above all endeavor to develop the student's ability to think; they must help him see that the objective of thinking is truth and that the ultimate goal of the educated man is truth in action.

The second value that endures in a changing world is a cultural value—beauty. The colleges have as one of their primary objectives—all too frequently neglected—the teaching of the student to have an understanding and appreciation of beauty in its manifold forms. If in the process the student can be led to creative activity of his own, so much the better, but such activity is not essential to an experience of beauty. It is particularly important that we try to develop such esthetic sensitivity in our students that they will no longer tolerate the drabness and the ugliness that surrounds our daily lives but rather to make color and beauty more pervasive in the new world that we are creating.

But in providing an "education," colleges must be concerned with more than the intellect and the emotional qualities that respond to beauty. The development of the intellect and the sharpening of the esthetic sense must be infused with moral and spiritual qualities. These the colleges cannot neglect. These also are values which endure regardless of the sweep of history and the changing conditions of the world. They must be reaffirmed in our time or mankind may indeed find itself not in any fabulous future but in hopeless chaos.

The moral value that is the goal of education may be summed up in the word "integrity." It goes beyond honesty and it implies courage. It must be admitted that colleges do not know well how to develop integrity; certainly there is no pat formula for it. It is undoubtedly less susceptible to direct teaching than is the ability to think and we know little enough of this process. Yet we must do our best to develop integrity in our students. It is a quality that is indispensable if a better and happier world is to come.

Finally there is spiritual value—and its objective can best be expressed as "love." The concept of love is the most important single contribution of the Christian tradition to our value system. Christ taught us to love God and to love our neighbor. And in this shrunken world, as I have pointed out, neighbor means man wherever he is, regardless of the color of his skin, the language he speaks, or the political system he adheres to.

Institutions of higher education, let it be understood, cannot alone inculcate the moral and spiritual virtues necessary for today's world and tomorrow's. But they have a major part in the process.

Truth, beauty, integrity, love—these are values that will endure so long as man survives. His way of life will change materially. But so long as man is man he will need to seek the truth and live by its dictates, to discover beauty and to infuse his life with its glory, to walk upright as a man of integrity and to expect his fellow men to do the same, and to learn how to live with God and with his neighbor—who is man everywhere—in accordance with those spiritual admonitions which, transcending the here and the now, endure through the ages.

It is given to teachers, whether in colleges or in the elementary and secondary schools, to help young people establish a life solidly constructed upon these enduring values. Theirs is the great task of our time. In no other profession are the opportunities so challenging. In no other job is the contribution that can be made to society so significant or so long-lasting. But to meet this challenge, to make this contribution, teachers have to be committed themselves to these enduring values and demonstrate them not just by what they say, but by what they do in their own lives. If they do so, then education will fulfill its great role, it will truly be the major factor in the avoidance of catastrophe and the achievement of the good life the future promises for all of mankind.

CITIZENSHIP RESPONSIBILITY IN EDUCATION [13]

GEORGE ROMNEY [14]

George Romney's name is durably associated with the production and marketing of the compact car. He has been president and chairman of the American Motors Corporation since 1954. But he is a man of many interests and enthusiasms, one of which is a concern over the citizen's role in strengthening the educational system. With characteristic forthrightness, he asserts that "in the field of education we have had a terrific amount of talk, but I think we have reached the point where we need some action." The accomplishments of the Detroit Citizens' Committee, of which Romney was chairman, underline this call for action.

The "almost terrifyingly earnest head of the American Motors Corporation," as A. H. Raskin called him in a recent issue of the New York *Times Magazine,* delivered this speech on February 15, 1960. The occasion was the meeting of the American Association of School Administrators at Atlantic City, New Jersey.

I consider it a great honor to be here with the distinguished guests and members of this audience. I think you hold a position of leadership second to none in the nation.

In 1941 the great Willow Run bomber plant was being dedicated on the outskirts of Detroit. And because the whole nation knew the importance of getting some bombers at that time, this was a national event. There were three distinguished speakers: Undersecretary of War Patterson talked for half an hour, and then the governor talked for an hour and then R. J. Thomas, president of the United Automobile Workers talked for half an hour. At that point the presiding officer introduced Mr. Henry Ford. Mr. Ford, in his eighties, toddled up to the microphone and said, "I can't talk, but I will do all I can," and toddled back.

[13] Text furnished by A. F. Wilson, assistant director of public relations, American Motors Corporation, with permission for this reprint.

[14] For biographical note, see Appendix; for reference to an earlier speech, see Cumulative Author Index.

Now, as a matter of fact, those were the most appropriate words that he could say on that occasion. There had been a terrific amount of talk in the pre-Pearl Harbor period, but not much action. And it was a time for action. I think in the field of education we have had a terrific amount of talk, but I think we have reached the point where we need some action.

Leadership Responsibility

I think that action is going to depend importantly upon your discharge of your leadership responsibility. The basis of our leadership responsibility in a free society goes back to the fact that we believe we are divinely created beings, that our Creator has endowed us with certain inalienable rights, and that as a result of those rights we have government by consent. In order to have government by consent, we have divided all forms of power. We have divided political power and economic power, and we have vested ultimate control of this society in the hands of the people.

I believe with Jefferson that the only safe depository for the ultimate control of society is the people themselves. And if we consider them not sufficiently enlightened to exercise that control with reasonable discretion, the answer is not to take it from them, but to educate them.

Under a free society where people exercise ultimate control, and properly exercise it, the people who can only individually be expert in one or two fields, depend upon leadership in other fields to determine the best things that can be done and to give them a choice.

I believe that that is your responsibility in the field of education. As the leaders in public education, you have the responsibility of seeing that programs are developed that permit the people to have a choice.

I think you have the responsibility of initiation and motivation, and inspiration. I am here today not because I am president of American Motors, but because the Superintendent of Schools in Detroit, Dr. Samuel Brownell, and his Board of

Education, initiated a program that resulted in my discharging some of my citizenship responsibility in the field of education.

My experiences convince me of the vital need for a new and higher expression of citizenship in education. Furthermore, we possess the means to achieve both. And by succeeding, I think we can build a new age in America that will take us well beyond past accomplishments of our own country or any other country.

America's Opportunity

While the Soviet Union, with a few scientific exceptions, and all other nations, are striving to duplicate our past results we have the exclusive opportunity as a nation to pioneer new levels, culturally, politically, economically, and socially.

Whether we do so depends primarily on our application to today's problems of the spiritual, social, and educational principles that made the United States the greatest nation in all history.

Whether we can do this depends on rising above our obsession with our present entrenched but partial material success— a success that has been over-emphasized by American industry to the detriment of our whole nation—and carving a vision of what can be, at home and around the world.

One of the most precious things we have lost is a sense of conviction. I think if there is any school administrator here that doesn't believe in the basic principles of a free society that I referred to at the start of this talk, then that administrator lacks the most essential ingredient of leadership in the field of public education.

Unfortunately, reports from people outside of our country and people from our country who have visited Russia tell us that the great difference is the difference of conviction and enthusiasm and dedication; that their people, old and young, have the dedication, the conviction and the enthusiasm that we once had, but no longer have.

As a matter of fact, Dr. Charles Malik, until a year ago president of the United Nations General Assembly, said the

American people don't even know their own traditions; they don't believe in them any longer.

We must never forget these facts: Every good and excellent thing stands moment by moment on the razor edge of danger and must be fought for. We never achieve a point which we can retain without continued effort. What we have already attained educationally and otherwise can only be retained with effort and struggle.

Second, it has been said that if any nation values anything more than freedom, it will lose its freedom. And the irony is if it is comfort and security it wants, it will lose them, too. I want to add that if it is peace and prosperity we want more than freedom, we will lose our freedom, and peace and prosperity too.

Walt Whitman has said that every fruition of success, no matter what, is followed by something to make necessary a still greater struggle. I think it is the success we have achieved in America, in the field of education and elsewhere, that confronts us with new problems that require a greater degree of effort and a greater degree of struggle than previously in the history of our country.

Realizing Our Opportunities

In the history of education, what are the successes calling for a greater struggle, and what are our means for success?

First, our early adoption of universal public education and equality of educational opportunity as national goals has produced an appreciation and use of both traditional pre-college liberal arts instruction, and vocational training. This combination of curriculum subjects is essential in meeting the goal of equal educational opportunity based on the widely varying capacities of children in both fields. Without both, how can each child be given the degree of mental development and practical training of which he is capable and which he is willing to achieve?

Second, our experience with the traditional "education by rote" method and the more recent progressive approach indicates both contain elements of successful teaching methods necessary to instruct children with widely varying aptitudes and capacities. Every one of us who has a family of children, of three or four or more—or two—is aware of the fact that each child varies. They respond differently to praise and discipline, and have to be dealt with on an individual basis.

Third, while our economic obsession has produced material success at the sacrifice of adequate interest in education, it has nevertheless provided the resources capable of financing not only the additional facilities and personnel for our lengthening educational program and increasing school population, but also the compensation levels needed to attract and hold capable teachers and administrators.

Fourth, the greater economic rewards given to other professions, and even to highly skilled workers, make it easy to arouse public support for the recognition and compensation deserved by the capable teacher or administrator. If those things didn't exist, it would be a tougher job.

Fifth, we are engaged in the greatest struggle for survival the world has ever seen, in the ideological field, the scientific field, the military, technological, the propaganda, and the political areas. This unprecedented world-wide struggle develops a need for highly educated and trained citizens that is greater than any previous need.

Again reverting to Dr. Malik—and I have read all the talks he has made in the last two or three years because I consider him the ablest non-American observer of America— he says we should prepare for the fact that the forces opposed to us possess the natural resources and the population resources, and the affinity with other cultural groups so they are going to surpass us in the purely material field. He says the only hope we have for winning this struggle for survival is to develop people with capacity and character greater than any other peoples on the face of the earth.

Sixth, whereas our educational programs were originally established for generations who were to establish American liberty and settle a continent, future American generations must be educated not only to achieve a new and higher age in America, but to assist peoples everywhere in establishing their own liberty and the economic means to pursue their personal development within their own culture.

Seventh, the desperate need of future generations for education vastly exceeding that of their forefathers cannot be satisfied through any influence less powerful than the wholehearted cooperation of free citizens in providing the necessary public support and parental participation.

Primary reliance on national leadership and Federal action could deprive our future educational programs of the public understanding and support that are essential to achieving state, community, and home attitudes needed for effective educational programs. We are fortunate to have state and local structures that can be used to change the grassroots attitudes about education, because those are the most important attitudes in a free society.

Eighth, there is growing public concern about the adequacy of our educational programs and the exercise of our citizenship responsibilities. Despite the comfort of our material abundance, American citizens increasingly are becoming disturbed. Samuel Lubell, who has been the most accurate prober of public attitude in the last several years in this country, in a survey about ten months ago said that the American public attitude was one of uneasiness, frustration, and helplessness. That growing concern provides the opportunity to undertake the struggle needed to launch dynamic community and state educational programs.

The Detroit School Committee

As I have already indicated, I am a product of such a program in the city of Detroit. Up until the fall of 1956 I was probably a typical parent and citizen. I had been so busy with business and church and other matters that I had been to two or three PTA meetings, looked at the children's report cards, and left the rest of it up to my wife and the teachers. I knew little about education, other than my own educational training. But I did know the basic importance of education.

In the fall of 1956 the chairman of the Detroit School Board and Dr. Brownell came to see me and said they had talked with all significant elements of the community about a citizens' study of educational needs in the city of Detroit. They wanted to know if I would serve as chairman of that committee.

Well, in the fall of 1956 American Motors stock was selling for $5 to $6 a share, and that meant the American people had little confidence in our survival, so it wasn't something I could answer immediately. I said I wanted to give it some thought.

As I gave it thought, the only conclusion I could come to was that I had to accept the responsibility, because I considered education our most important public service and citizenship responsibility, and more important than anything in the life of a citizen other than his church and his home.

I put down at that time my basic convictions. I said: I believe public education is one of the major and indispensable reasons for America's rapid rise to world leadership. I believe only the educated can be free, that education makes a people easier to be led constructively, but difficult to drive; easy to govern, but impossible to enslave. I believe education should have as its objectives the formation of character and citizenship, and the development of individual intellects and talents.

I believe ignorance is the obstacle to progress, and knowledge is essential to human happiness.

Against that background, I said yes.

The Detroit study succeeded because the motivators of it, Dr. Brownell and the Board of Education, understood the American society and the American principles. And they set it up on the basis of sound democratic principles.

They asked all 280 of us on the city-wide committee and eight regional committees in the vast Detroit metropolitan area, to serve as citizens, and to subordinate our economic, political, and other affiliations to our citizenship responsibility. That is something desperately needed, not only in education but in other fields in America.

They did another thing. They said this group would be free to probe any area of the Detroit educational program, and that all they wanted to know was what this citizenship group thought the city needed in the decade ahead. They provided some facilities and some staff, but we raised our own operating funds from representative groups through the community.

Winning Community Approval

Then, as a committee, we followed sound procedures. We avoided the fatal mistake of starting out by expressing our biases and our convictions based on partial information. We decided we should first define the problems in the five fields of curriculum, personnel, school plant, finance, and community relations. And having defined the problems and the issues so that we agreed on what they were, we decided we would then collect all the available facts on the Detroit school system and on any other school system through the nation that could help us determine needs and what could be done.

That simple process reduces the differences between people to a minimum level and brings them to the discussion of solutions and recommendations against a background of common factual information. That resulted in this case.

We put the facts about the Detroit school system and other school systems in writing, and agreed on what the provable facts were before we discussed future needs. When we came to the discussion of future needs, we made another decision which I think was important.

The community was divided and confused. An attempt to get moderate increases in school revenues had failed in 1957 by a split vote because one minority group had used partial information to confuse the people. We decided we should limit recommendations to those on which we were in practically unanimous agreement. We decided that we should unite the community behind those things that clearly needed to be done rather than to argue about controversial matters that would take more time to settle. And we agreed on 183 recommendations, including 57 in curriculum, and 57 in personnel, the two largest areas in terms of the number of recommendations.

Then we made another decision that was fundamental to our success. We decided to ask the newspapers and the radio and television stations to sit down with us and tell us how we could communicate these facts to the people of the community on a basis that would enable them to understand what the facts were and what our recommendations were. We put up to them their citizenship responsibility of helping to determine the program of communication. They said we ought to do it on an organized basis—break it down into pieces, and to present it over an extended period of time, so people could digest parts of it.

That was done and they all cooperated with the result that when we got through with the submission of our report and recommendations, the public had a basic concept of what was involved.

That completed the job of our committee. We made our report and turned it over to the Board of Education.

At that point the Board of Education set up another committee of a thousand citizens under Federal Judge Arthur Lederle, to secure public action on the revenue proposals. These were a three-mill increase in the school tax, and a $60 million bond issue, much larger proposals than had been defeated three to one in the spring of 1957. And they were approved.

Since the report was issued, the School Board has approved 141 of the recommendations. Five more were approved with slight modification, and the remaining 37 are being studied further. None have been rejected.

Citizen interest has been aroused. Our recommendations included proposals for citizen participation in connection with the planning of school buildings, development of equal educational opportunity in the community, future financial requirements, curriculum programs—many areas where citizen groups were recommended as participants in developing the programs of the city.

The extent to which citizen interest has continued is difficult to measure exactly, but both Dr. Brownell and I know it has been increased materially.

I think one evidence of that is the fact that three Detroit newspapers and the radio and television stations are dealing at greatly increased length and frequency with school needs. As a matter of fact, one of our papers has a reporter here today and she specializes on educational matters. And the other two papers have reporters who specialize on educational matters because they believe the people of the city are interested in educational development. One of the radio stations has assigned a man full time to educational news.

Teacher Compensation and Status

There are some things we didn't do. We didn't put teachers on a merit basis consistent with professional status. That was controversial.

As John Millis stated in the *Journal of Higher Education* in 1957:

Teaching should, nay must occupy a position of qualitative importance shared only with that of the ministry. The physician can preserve the health of the body, the dentist the health of the teeth, the engineer our standard of living. But the teacher deals with mind and spirit and therefore can preserve that which makes man human rather than animal, free rather than slave, governor rather than governed.

It is my personal view that while much attention has been devoted, with much justified sympathy, to teaching as the underdog profession, the fundamental status of teachers is much better than they themselves believe it is. And I also believe that much of the blame for any loss in stature that has occurred must be borne by members of the teaching profession.

When teachers engage in public debate about whether they should or should not be in school a few minutes before class begins and remain a few minutes after it ends, they hardly give the impression they are as dedicated as many of us remember our teachers used to be.

Let me say this to you: My children, and the children I went to school with, were influenced in terms of the basic American principles that I enunciated not so much by what the teachers said in the classroom as by the evidence of their basic belief and acceptance of those principles. I have found that children are very quick to detect when teachers and others believe things and when they don't believe things and are just mouthing them.

The concept that the group can increase its professional stature by accepting wage standards based on time in grade rather than contribution also does not ring with an air of consistency in the public mind, which associates this type of concept with an entirely different type of economic function in our society.

The impression also has been created in some quarters that in their legitimate fight for higher standards some teachers are seeking more reward for less endeavor and, in a sense, lower teaching productivity.

I might say in Detroit in many areas the starting salaries of teachers are fully comparable with the beginning salary rates in most of industry. My twenty-seven-year-old son-in-law is starting work today for a big corporation at a lower salary than he could get by starting in as a teacher in the city of Detroit. Teachers' salaries do lag as experience increases, but some of this lag may be due to the conflict in salary objectives between what is normal for a professional group and what is established as a pattern for a factory group doing uniform work for uniform pay.

Let me state some of these things more clearly and sharply.

I personally do not believe that teachers will ever achieve the status of a profession until they approach the whole question on a professional basis. I do not believe they can ever do it by picking up the collective bargaining tactics of people who are not professional in character.

Political Action by Citizens

Now, a second thing the Detroit Citizens' Committee did not do was to resolve the basic long-range financial requirements. And that was because the problem was metropolitan in character, and state-wide in character. It involved more than just the city of Detroit. But the Detroit Citizens' Committee work did inspire a type of state-wide citizens' program that I believe will be capable of meeting the long-range needs. The financial crisis that we have had in the state of Michigan grew out of excessive partisanship and citizen apathy and the neglect of political affairs by citizens, with the result that minority pressure groups have moved in and dominated both political parties. The political situation in Michigan is one that can be accurately described as being on the verge of political bankruptcy, a deadlock between the two major economic groups dominating the two major political groups.

Under those circumstances, some of us who were engaged in the citizens' study on Detroit school needs decided that the same democratic principles could be used to stimulate citizen interest in the state's problems, including education, and create an influence in the state greater than any minority influence. That is what the two political parties are currently, because there aren't enough citizens participating in them to make them majority influences. They are minority influences because of citizen political apathy.

We have created "Citizens for Michigan" as a means of creating a vehicle through which the citizens of the state, regardless of party or economic affiliation, can determine the state's needs on the basis of their citizenship responsibility rather than on the basis of which economic group they belong to.

Let me ask you this question: When American citizens in the exercise of their citizenship are actuated primarily on the basis of their economic affiliation, what is the essential difference between Americanism and communism? To me that is economic determinism. I am convinced that the citizens of this country have got to reassert their citizenship responsibility, which is superior to their economic or other responsibility, if we are going to meet the problems in our communities and states.

Meeting Our Citizenship Responsibility

I am convinced that meeting our educational needs depends on recapturing a sense of dedication to our national destiny and educating our children to take a world-wide approach to its fulfillment. We must inspire faith in our traditions and institutions, and impart that faith through our schools and elsewhere.

We must recapture our sense of purpose nationally and educationally, and instill it in our children by our conduct and our attitude more than our words.

Second, we need a greater degree of personal dedication to that educational program by superintendents, principals, and teachers—a dedication so great that it will not permit the material to dominate, divide, and defeat. The material can always be shaped by the spiritual and the ethical and the moral.

Third, we need acceptance by public officials, including school boards and citizen groups, of the primary responsibility for supplying the money needed, and arousing the community and parental support that are indispensable.

Fourth, we need recognition that every child varies in his intellectual and vocational potential and that achieving the maximum of both should be the objective of all who are concerned with a school.

Fifth, accepting the responsibilities of parents, churches and others for the training of children, we need to recognize the inevitable necessity of educators coping with the deficiencies in these areas, with ready willingness to overcome them to the extent possible.

It is relatively easy, I believe, to plan and organize an ideal educational system. But the problems arise from the fact that education involves the greatest of all variables—children, and human institutions.

With a clear national educational purpose, a successful educational program is the product of responsible parenthood, wholehearted citizenship, effective use of democratic principles and processes, capable and respected educational personnel making effective use of available and—whenever possible—adequate facilities, all united on a purposeful basis of community support.

I am convinced that young people want meaning in their lives, and I don't think they are getting it. I believe they want us to give them great meanings and great objectives, and great convictions. These they must have if they are to preserve the good and excellent from the past and take advantage of the greatest era in all history that lies ahead, an era that will be won or lost on the basis of the quality of their intellect and their character. These responses on their part present a challenge that depends primarily in my judgment on your leadership in your community and in your state.

TO HAVE AND NOT TO HOLD [15]

ROBERT J. McCRACKEN [16]

This sermon was delivered by the pastor of the Riverside Church, in New York City, on November 1, 1959. Although it contains a specific call for pledges to assist in the work of Riverside Church, the basic appeal is universal.

Dr. McCracken's presentation is a fine example of speech composition. The organization of materials is compact, allowing for prompt and smooth movement through the succession of ideas. The illustrative material is apt and interesting. The style is clear, providing for swift and easy understanding.

Matthew 6:14-21. *Do not lay up for yourselves treasures on earth, where moth and rust consume and where thieves break in and steal, but lay up for yourselves treasures in heaven, where neither moth nor rust consumes and where thieves do not break in and steal; for where your treasure is, there will your heart be also.*

It is a solemn moment when, standing in church before the altar of God, a bridegroom says to his bride, "I take thee to my wedded wife, to have and to hold from this day forward." In token of his vow he puts a ring on the third finger of her left hand. At one time people believed that that finger contained a nerve that ran straight to the heart, and the heart was thought to be the seat of the affections.

To have and to hold! It is a time-honored phrase and one that applies to much more than matrimony. All the finest human relationships should be governed by it. "The friends thou hast, and their adoption tried, grapple them to thy soul with hooks of steel." What is true of friendship is also true of cardinal virtues like justice, fortitude, hope, faith. Part of the art of living is to treasure them, keep hold of them, never let them go.

[15] Text furnished by Dr. McCracken, with permission to reprint.
[16] For biographical note, see Appendix; for reference to an earlier speech, see Cumulative Author Index.

It is not true of money. Jesus warned us against piling it up.
The warning has been needed in generation after generation,
and all the great sages and moralists have joined Jesus in utter-
ing it. They cannot be said to have been too successful. The
passion to possess and accumulate is uncommonly strong in
human nature. The prevailing tendency, interest and preoccupa-
tion of society is to promote the making of money. Ruskin
called it the first of all English games but the English have no
monopoly of it. The dominant vice of our time may well be
avarice. The acquisitive instinct is encouraged; creative and spiritual instincts are chronically undernourished. Money is always
forthcoming for the making of money but difficult to obtain for
the needs of the most needy and for good and deserving causes.

"The occupation which gives a man most pleasure is making
money." That sentence has a modern ring. Does it surprise you
to learn that it dates from the year B.C. 570? Mention the Gold
Rush and most of us think of California in 1849 and 1850. Yet
when and where have men not yearned to strike it rich? The
offices of the Ford Foundation were first set up on an estate in
Pasadena, California, and before very long the staff had nick-
named the estate Itching Palms. Dwight Macdonald has defined
the Ford Foundation as "a large body of money completely surrounded by people who want some." In similar vein a minister
has recently been complaining that his congregation may not turn
up at prayer meeting, but they will all be there if and when their
names are called on "Stop the Music" or "Break the Bank."

Jesus dealt often with the passion to possess and accumulate
money. We should be clear in that connection about one thing.
He did warn of the grip it can take on the heart, of the menace
it can be to character, how it can harden the sympathies, create a
false sense of security, distort one's scale of values, bind and
blind the soul. But He never taught that money in itself was
evil. What He assailed was the greedy, grasping, covetous instinct which makes acquisition the goal of life and sees in money
an end in itself. What He concentrated attention on was the
attitude adopted towards it and the use made of it. Dives was
condemned, not because he was wealthy, but because he did not

share his wealth with the needy. The rich young ruler was told to go and sell all he had, not because the possession of private property is wrong, but because his riches were coming between him and God.

To have and not to hold is then a Christian principle. It is a reminder that *there are things money cannot buy.* An old proverb runs, "Beauty is potent, money is omnipotent." Proverbs, however, are often no more than half-truths. To be sure, money is tremendously powerful; even so there are sharp limits to what it can do and there are things it cannot even begin to do. "Money," said Josh Billings, "will buy a pretty good dog, but it won't buy the wag of his tail." We Americans are puzzled by our unpopularity overseas. We pour billions into foreign aid programs. We are slow to appreciate that money is of little avail when it is a matter of winning friendship and devotion. The fact is the best things in life are not to be had for money. You can't shop for them in Tiffany's. They are not on the market in Wall Street or the Stock Exchange—nobleness of character, a tranquil conscience, peace of mind, and that greatest boon of all, the forgiveness and fellowship of God.

Ours being a money culture we need to be reminded of the things that matter more than money. When Cynthia Asquith became James Barrie's personal secretary and set about tidying up his desk she found in it a bundle of uncashed checks, which added together came to £1700. Do you know Barrie's story? Did you ever see him? I did once; it was on the day he was given the freedom of the city of Edinburgh. Who that saw it can forget that sad, pathos-ridden face? Who that heard it can forget that hauntingly wistful voice? He was a success as an author and playwright. He made money, piles of money, but those uncashed checks lying about his desk tell their own story. There are treasures no money can buy.

To have and not to hold is a Christian principle because *we have so much and other have so little.* Ever since I traveled through the East I have had to ask myself some questions over and over again. Why was I born into a Christian home and not into one darkened by ignorance, superstition and fear? Why was

I privileged to go to school and university when millions in Africa, Asia and South America can neither read nor write? Why have I never known poverty or hunger, real hunger, when in India millions go to bed at night with only a single meal a day? What is the answer to those questions? There is no answer other than that of the New Testament, "Freely you have received, freely give." The only justification of privilege is the opportunity it affords of service. To any one rich in brains and money, well fed, well clothed, well housed, well educated, the only thing to say is: There is no reason why you should have these things and not somebody else. You must make a reason for them. You must justify them by the use to which you put them, by scorning to hoard them selfishly, by magnanimously sharing them.

Selfish plenty while abject poverty exists is an unmitigated evil. It creates gulfs between men. It is a denial of brotherhood. It shrinks the soul of rich and poor alike. It was the sin for which Dives went to hell. It was the sin that led Peter to say to Ananias, "Your money perish with you." When Carlyle awoke to the absurd, irrational inequalities of England's economic life, when it came home to him that there were single individuals whose incomes were equal to those of some seven or eight thousand others, he demanded as an Old Testament prophet might have demanded: "What do those highly favored individuals *do* to society for their wages?—*Kill partridges.* Can this last? No, by the soul that is in man it cannot, and will not, and shall not!" In our own day, facing a not dissimilar situation, Albert Schweitzer was not content, putting pen to paper, to explode in righteous indignation. He saw Africa lying like a beggar on Europe's doorstep and the sight carried him there to found a hospital. Not long ago he was asked why he left Europe to go and bury himself in Africa. He replied: "The answer is quite simple. I saw we had so much, and they had so little, that I felt I ought to go and take them some of our blessings." When I see young people in this city beginning to carve out careers for themselves I want to say to them: Don't let your attitude be, The world owes me a living and I am going to get it. Instead let it be, I owe the world a life, and I am going to give it.

To have and not to hold is a Christian principle because, *however much money we may acquire and accumulate, we can't take it with us.* Death is the great leveler. When death comes the money that means so much to us is of no use to us. Current coin here, it counts for nothing on the other side. At the bar of final judgment it may be a liability, not an asset. After telling the parable of the rich fool, Jesus left His hearers in no doubt of its point. The whole business of life is to become "rich toward God." "Get yourselves purses that never grow old, inexhaustible treasure in heaven." Henry van Dyke wrote a story about a wealthy man who had a palatial residence on earth and was taken aback to find when he reached heaven that he had only a tiny hut. "You see," he was told, "you didn't send us enough material to build anything better." To hold on to money in selfish, miserly fashion is to become mean-minded, spiritually deformed and therefore spiritually doomed. The great use of money is to spend it on something that will outlast it. It is to exchange what you can't keep for what you can't lose.

A father and mother, humble farmer folk, sent their son to college and sacrificed to keep him there. He worked hard, won prizes and at length was about to graduate. They went to the ceremony and took their places, self-consciously, among the commencement throng. Their son was salutatorian, and they beamed with pride over the applause that broke out as he sat down. But when the applause continued on and on until the boy had to bow a second time in acknowledgment, the father could keep silent no longer. Nudging his wife he said, "Mary, by all odds, that's the best crop we ever raised."

To have and not to hold is a Christian principle because God has the Supreme claim on our money. It is not ours to keep or to spend as we please; it is given to us in trust for His service; we are stewards, not sole owners and proprietors. The proper handling of money is an essential part of honest religion. If our religion does not affect and direct both the making and the spending of our money it has not come to grips with the realities of our everyday existence. When David was dedicating the offerings which had been brought to Jerusalem for the building of

the temple, he said: "All things come of Thee, and of Thine
own have we given Thee . . . O Lord our God, all this store
that we have prepared to build Thee an house for Thine holy
name cometh of Thine hand, and is all Thine own." A grateful
and adoring congregation were only giving back to God what
was His already, by sovereign right. Paul, in his speech at
Athens, voiced the same conviction: "He giveth to all life, and
breath, and all things." On another occasion the Apostle re-
buked the smugness of some of his fellow-Christians by putting
to them the blunt questions: "Who maketh thee to differ from
another? And what hast thou that thou didst not receive?" The
teaching of Jesus is shot through with the same tremendous
assumptions. In the parables of the talents and the pounds where
He deals explicitly with the use to which people put their money,
the emphasis is on the need of wise and faithful stewardship.
It is God's money, He says, not ours. God has invested it in us,
and like all investors He looks for a return. What dividend does
He get from us? About men and women who regarded their
money, not as their private property to be disposed of as they
pleased but as a sacred trust from God, Jesus was quick to say,
"Well done, good and faithful servant."

To have and not to hold because there are things that matter
more than money, because we have so much and others have so
little, because the great use of money is to spend it on something
that will outlast it, because God has the supreme claim on all we
are and have—on those grounds I ask your support for the work
to be done here in 1960. The new south wing will be open in
1960. It has cost us nothing to build. It will cost us nothing to
operate and maintain the building. But the work done for God
and man in the building—the expanding church school, the new
program features, the new community services, for example, an
ordained minister on our staff to lead and minister to our
Spanish-speaking constituency, the new FM radio station—that
will be costly. We shall require $320,000 in contributions, which
is $30,000 more than we required for 1959. To raise that
amount will mean increased pledges from each of us. I cannot
believe that any member or friend of Riverside will complain on

that score. Nothing can stir the human heart so deeply to humility and generosity as to be benefited and enriched beyond all expectation or merit. What Mr. Rockefeller has done will surely inspire you and me to do far more than we have ever done before. This congregation has been confronted with the supreme opportunity of its life.

The sum of $240 million has been asked for the Saturn rocket project for next year. When the Aqueduct race track was opened in September 42,473 persons wagered on the first day $3,430,765. The per capita betting on that day was $80.77. More than nine billion dollars a year are spent in this country on liquor. More than four billion dollars a year are spent on tobacco. Think of what is spent on cars and clothes. People will spend money freely on what they want. How much are we who call ourselves Christians ready and eager to spend for the Church of Christ? The best thing anybody can do for the future of the world is to help increase the influence of Christ within it. It is for this you are being asked to make a generous pledge today. The amount of your pledge to your church is the acid test of your faith.

What should that amount be? The Old Testament is explicit in its reply. It should be a tenth of all we have. The canvass literature suggests that at least we should make it one dollar per week for each thousand dollars of annual income. The New Testament soars above all such arithmetical calculation. Its challenge is to a loyalty and a service and a sacrifice that knows no limits. Breathtaken by the grace of God revealed in the life and death of Christ, its writers feel the constraint of the divine love to such a degree that no offering ever seems to them adequate and no service worthy.

Dr. J. H. Jowett used to tell of a woman in a little village who spent herself unwearyingly and recklessly in the service of God and man. When she died and was laid to rest in the village cemetery the epitaph over her grave read, "She Hath Done What She Couldn't." Love at its best is always like that—ready to go the second mile, not afraid of the heart getting the better of the head, generous to the point of reckless extravagance, with an

enthusiasm and an abandon that gives and spends and can't hold
back. "Love's strength standeth on love's sacrifice." May the
God of love inspire in all of us, members and friends of Riverside, a love like that.

> Teach us, Good Lord, to serve Thee as Thou
>   deservest,
> To give and not to count the cost,
> To fight and not to heed the wounds,
> To work and not to seek for rest,
> To labor and not to ask for any reward
>   save that of knowing that we do
>   Thy will.   Amen.

"HOW WOULD YOU HAVE US?" [17]

Rufus E. Clement [18]

World peace and disarmament excepted, perhaps no issue in American life was more prominently in public view during the past year than civil rights. After some fifty word-heavy days of debate, the Senate approved a bill, the second since Reconstruction days, intended to help guarantee the voting rights of Negroes. During this time, racial tensions in the South increased. Student demonstrations and sit-downs, largely against segregated lunch counters in the South, gave dramatic impetus to the drive for an integrated America.

The nature of the crisis was set forth concisely by the president of Atlanta University, Dr. Rufus E. Clement, in a speech at the Denver Theater Auditorium, Denver, Colorado, on March 27, 1960. This was the annual convocation of the United Negro College Fund. On the platform with Dr. Clement were the presidents of thirty of the thirty-three member colleges of the Fund. Dr. John A. Hannah, president of Michigan State University and chairman of the United States Commission on Civil Rights, also addressed the meeting.

In the words of a prominent Negro poet, addressed to the American people,

> How would you have us?
> Strong sinews in your arms
> Or tightening chains about your feet? [19]

We meet here tonight in Denver in a time of crisis. One has but to turn on TV, or listen to the radio, or to pick up the *Rocky Mountain News* or the Denver *Post* (or any newspaper worthy of the name published in this and in other nations of the world) to realize the state in which we find ourselves today. It is disturbing to me and, I am sure, to you, that the Congress of the United States has now, for more than six weeks, been debating the question whether full civil rights and the guarantees thereof shall be extended to one large portion of the population.

[17] Text furnished by Dr. Clement, with permission for this reprint.
[18] For biographical note, see Appendix.
[19] A paraphrase from James Weldon Johnson's "We to America" in *Saint Peter Relates an Incident* (New York: Viking, 1935).

We are disturbed that men in the debates which have gone on in the Senate of the United States have not always told the full story; to say nothing of the actual situations as they certainly exist in one section of the country and as some of us here tonight know exist in our own states.

You have been reading the newspapers even as of this day and you have seen many and regular accounts of a new development in American life: the so-called "sit-in" protests by students in cafés and lunch rooms throughout many of the states which are represented by institutions and their presidents here on this platform tonight. In fact, Mr. Trent did not tell you that one of the presidents (the one who was missing, to whom he referred) had to leave this group to go back home to his city of Nashville because of certain situations which arose there subsequent to the time when he left for this meeting. I have tonight shown my colleagues from Atlanta a newspaper clipping which sets forth some things which have occurred, which we did not think would occur, after we left the city last Wednesday. The end is not yet in sight; no one knows for certain what will happen tomorrow.

I am disturbed about this and I am quite sure that all of the presidents are also. I believe that you are, too. For what is happening represents more than an effort of a few Negro students and some sympathizers to get a cup of coffee, a sandwich, or a hamburger at some local stand. What actually is the case is that we see now the wholesale protestation, on the part of this younger generation, against conditions which have surrounded their elders for many years and against which they have, of course, made protest and fortunately seen some progress made. But "progress" in the eyes and in the minds of these young people which has not been sufficient and which has not been speedily achieved. So we find ourselves today concerned with these student situations, these demonstrations, these developments which are asking for more than food, which are asking that suffrage, housing, job opportunities, transportation opportunities and facilities, hospitalizations, recreation and all of the whole gamut of public services be accorded them equally along with the major portion of the American population.

These young people have gone about this protestation, for the most part, in a sane, orderly, non-violent manner. They are not attempting to take anything from anybody else. They are simply attempting to win for themselves all of those rights and privileges, as well as the responsibilities, which are vouchsafed to all citizens in the Constitution of the United States and in the Constitutions of the states themselves—rights which, except for voting, are guaranteed and accorded even to every foreigner in our midst if his face is not dark or his hair not curly.

We are met at a time when there have been threats. There are currently threats—of my own state I know I can speak—that the public school system will be closed rather than to have the integration of a single Negro pupil in any public school in the entire state. We don't know yet what is going to develop but we do know that Georgia, Alabama, Louisiana, South Carolina, and Mississippi have set themselves adamantly against the acceptance of the decisions of the Supreme Court of the United States in the school cases. We are indeed fortunate tonight that we have as our guest and as another speaker on this program a great American who represents you and many like you and many millions of people in this nation who do believe that the republic should grant to all of its citizens full citizenship rights and should not have any second-class citizens left in this domain.

We are met at a time when crisis certainly presses in upon us in the international picture. The Geneva Disarmament Conference was described today in an article in the Denver *Post* as perhaps the most serious international conference of this generation—laying the groundwork for the Summit talks which will occur later, trying to make progress in perhaps one of the most difficult areas of international cooperation in the world today. Are we to see ourselves blown into eternity because peoples of the world cannot sit down together and decide that new technological developments should be used for peaceful means rather than for destructive purposes? I had the privilege last week, with a small committee which went to the White House for another purpose, of sitting for more than a half hour with the President of the United States. After we had in five minutes finished the task which we had gone in to perform, we had the pleasure of having the President, for more than thirty minutes, tell us many of the things (off the record) which had occurred during his two recent "Journeys to Understanding." [20] As we sat there and talked to him and asked questions and got replies, we could appreciate his anxiety that America would not find itself isolated in this present struggle for freedom and world peace. We noted the great emphasis which he put always, wherever he was, on peace and freedom and not just peace alone. You will recall that on the same day that we were there, he made a statement with regard to our domestic situation and what should be done here, recognizing that this also presented a critical and a crucial area for these United States.

We have been disturbed, all of us, by what is happening now in South Africa: that troops for any reason whatsoever would fire volley after volley into groups, large numbers of defenseless men, women, and children in their home country as they protested having to carry identity passes whenever they left their own homes in their own lands. This is the situation; we are confronted nationally and internationally with a time which calls for planning and which calls for cool, calculated solutions.

The colleges which we represent here tonight bring to the present situation certain instruments, certain talents which can be used, have been used, and we pray to God will be used more, in the solutions of the problems which some people in my own area have denominated and agreed upon in their own conservative minds as being insoluble. We do not agree with that conclusion. We represent "Colleges for Negroes." Not "Colleges for Negroes" because we would not have other people

[20] The President's official remarks on these journeys, "The European Trip" and "Peace and Friendship, in Freedom," are reprinted in the first section of this book.

study on our campuses, but "Colleges for Negroes" because traditionally at the end of the war, the Civil War, beginning at Lincoln University in Pennsylvania in 1854 and running down through the years, we began as citadels. We began as places to which Negro students, recently freed, and later the sons and daughters of ex-slaves and still later, in another generation "Americans all," could go freely; first for elementary education—because we represented the earliest attempts at education of the freedmen—and later, for higher education, in one great part of these United States. We represent the private colleges of this group: thirty-three institutions with freedom to think, to teach, to speak; thirty-three institutions located near to the population which they were founded to serve, not restricting their services to these people but open to all, but mainly used by these people because they are available and because they welcome all students.

We believe that we have in the past made significant contributions to American life. I will not take time to attempt to call any roll of leaders, living or dead, who have been educated in these institutions. You will recall I have already said that for many years these were the only institutions to which Negroes in the southern part of the United States could be admitted for higher education—and when I say higher education I mean anything above the elementary school level. I dare say that most of the men and women you see on this stage behind me, excluding the student group, received their high school education in private institutions because there were no public schools of even high school stature to which they would be admitted in their own states when they came along. You must remember that, when you judge the progress which has been made by the American Negro. You must remember that when you see the present struggle of the young Negro to have every educational opportunity which is open to anybody alse also available to him.

We have, we believe, made real contributions to American life. We think that we are presently making contributions as signal, if not more so. Higher education, of course, is the first field in which we make contributions. But we also make contributions in the field of interracial understanding and racial amity. The institutions which are represented here—these thirty-three—have almost without exception boards of trustees made up of citizens of both the white and Negro groups. Our faculties are mixed and many of our student groups include more than Negroes—we have white Americans (northern and southern), and people from foreign countries. But we also, living and situated in the South, provide opportunities in which all types of interracial committees and meetings making for good will and understanding can meet in an atmosphere of mutual confidence and friendship.

We are more than this. We are, I believe, in our training of people who serve the United States of America, testaments to American democracy. I could give you a long list—and many of my colleagues could add to even this list that I would present —of American Negroes now being used around the world in order to present as living examples the American idea that people of all cultures and of all races have opportunities in America. Perhaps not as many as they should—and the State Department does not argue that yet—but certainly that they can represent the United States of America. In some areas of the world—in the darker nations, the uncommitted nations—they can represent the United States better than many other people of the other group. The American image abroad among the two hundred million uncommitted peoples, depends a great deal upon the image, the picture, which the American Negro presents. But these colleges train not only people who are testaments of American democracy abroad. I would say more than that: these colleges train people who will test American democracy here at home. For it is my sanguine conclusion that upon its treatment of the Negro American democracy eventually stands or falls.

The philosophical base upon which these thirty-three institutions build their work and carry it on is very simple. We believe that religion is at the center of education and therefore the center of all life. All except three of these institutions— Hampton, Tuskegee and my own institution, Atlanta University—

have a very direct and a very close religious affiliation and church relationship.   The three of us, I'm quite sure, have as much of religion at the center of our activities as do even the theological seminaries represented in this group.   We believe that the acceptance of the Golden Rule in an individual life is certainly more important than the successful mastery of the three R's.   We believe, further, that education is good for all people and that every individual should have an attempt to receive, an opportunity to get, as much education as his own individual abilities and talents would warrant.   We feel that the educated man is more likely to make a constructive approach to human problems than is the ignorant man and so we take every man as far as we can, as far as our resources permit, and give him as much education as we possibly can afford.   We have four goals if you will let me mention them and bring them down to just four.   I would say that they are these: we are interested in training people of character, of intelligence, of industry and culture.   We feel that, as we do our jobs, if we achieve these four ends perhaps in that order: character, intelligence, industry and culture, we will certainly have done a good job and we certainly will be worthy of continued history and continued support.

There is a final philosophical basis for our work and that is our belief that every human being is made in the image of God and, therefore, that human dignity and individual worth are things to be highly considered.

In conclusion, I would have you remember that these colleges are training students for "inclusion" in American life. Ours is no "Separatist" movement.   We are not training leaders for a fifty-first state.   We are training people who want to contribute to America.   These colleges desire and hope and work for a stronger America.   We do not believe that America can afford to ignore, to ill-train, to cast aside, one tenth of its strength in the decisive decade which is in front of us.   To do so, in our opinion, would be most disastrous.   These colleges teach loyalty to the highest and finest ideals of this republic. We, too, sing "America."

I think that this was never so strongly borne in upon me, personally, as when one month ago today, the twenty-seventh of February, I was sitting before my television screen watching the Squaw Valley telecast of the hockey game between the teams representing the Soviet Union and the United States of America. Finally when the decisive goal, hockey goal, had been scored by an American—and this to my mind meant that we would win one of the three gold medals which we got out of the Winter Olympics and that in our direct competition with the USSR at another point we had come off victorious—I found my elation mounting so high that I suddenly discovered that I was standing, and to my utter amazement there were tears streaming down my face. As this happened, I stopped and my other self said to me, Are you a fool? Why do you weep? Why, why, why are *you* so glad? There isn't a single Negro on the Winter Olympics team. These are not your people, this is the United States of America and has nothing to do with you. And just as suddenly I put down all of this riotous, turgid voice within me and said, This *is* my team, this is *America,* I *am represented there, this is my country also.*

> Honest work for today,
> Honest hope for tomorrow
> Are these worth nothing
> Save the hands they make weary, the hearts they leave dreary?
> Hush! The seven-fold heavens are telling:
> He that overcometh will all things inherit!"

"How would you have us?"

APPENDIX

BIOGRAPHICAL NOTES

AKAKA, ABRAHAM KAHIKINA (1917-   ). Born, Honolulu, Hawaii; student, University of Hawaii, 1934-37; A.B., Illinois Wesleyan University, 1939; B.D., Chicago Theological Seminary, 1943; D.D., Chicago Theological Seminary, 1958; L.H.D., Salem College, 1959; pastor, West Kauai Larger Parish Council, 1943-45; Kahului Union Church, Kaahumanu Church, Waihee Church, Keawalai Church, Waikapu Church, Island of Maui, 1945-54; Haili Church, Hilo, 1954-57; Kawaiahao Church, Honolulu, 1957-   .

BOWLES, CHESTER (1901-   ). Born, Springfield, Massachusetts; Choate School, 1919; B.S., Yale University, 1924; LL.D., Oberlin College, 1957; reporter, Springfield *Republican,* 1924-25; partner in advertising firm, 1929-41; director, Office of Price Administration, 1943-46; member, War Production Board and Petroleum Council for War, 1943-46; director, Office of Economic Stabilization, 1946; American delegate to UNESCO, 1946; international chairman of campaign for United Nations Appeal for Children, 1947-48; special assistant to Trygve Lie, United Nations, 1947-48; governor of Connecticut, 1949-51; ambassador to India and Nepal, 1951-53; United States House of Representatives (Democrat, Connecticut) 1959-   ); author, *Tomorrow Without Fear,* 1946; *Ambassador's Report,* 1954; *The New Dimensions of Peace,* 1955; *American Politics in a Revolutionary World,* 1956; *Africa's Challenge to America,* 1956. (See also *Current Biography: 1957.*)

CLEMENT, RUFUS EARLY (1900-   ). Born, Salisbury, North Carolina; A.B., Livingstone College, 1919; B.D., Garrett Biblical Institute, 1922; A.M., Northwestern University, 1922, Ph.D. 1930; D.C.L., University of Liberia, 1956; L.H.D.,

Virginia Union University, 1958; instructor of history, Livingstone College, 1922-25; professor of history and dean, Livingstone College, 1925-31; dean, Louisville Municipal College for Negroes, 1931-37; president, Atlanta University, 1937- ; director, Georgia Commission on Inter-racial Cooperation, 1937-44; Alumni Award of Merit, Northwestern University, 1948; executive committee, United Negro College Fund; member, Phi Beta Kappa; member, officer, many civic and educational organizations. (See also *Current Biography: 1946.*)

DEAN, VERA MICHELES (1903-   ). Born, Petrograd, Russia; came to United States, 1919; A.B., Radcliffe College, 1925; A.M., Yale University, 1926, Ph.D., 1928; honorary degrees from several institutions; with Foreign Policy Association, 1931-   , editor and research director, 1938-   ; visiting professor, Smith College, 1952-54; director, Non-Western Civilizations Program, University of Rochester; author, *United States and Russia,* 1948; *Europe and the United States,* 1950; *Foreign Policy Without Fear,* 1953; *New Patterns of Democracy in India,* 1959. (See also *Current Biography: 1943.*)

DOUB, GEORGE COCHRAN (1902-   ). Born, Cumberland, Maryland; A.B., Johns Hopkins University, 1923; LL.B., University of Maryland, 1926; admitted to Maryland bar, 1926; assistant general solicitor, Western Maryland Railway Company, 1928-30, general attorney, 1930-34; partner in law firms, 1934-53; lieutenant commander, United States Naval Reserve, World War II; director, Mental Hygiene Society of Maryland, 1947-52; United States Attorney, District of Maryland, 1953-56; assistant attorney general of the United States in charge of the Civil Division, 1956-   .

EISENHOWER, DWIGHT DAVID (1890-   ). Born, Denison, Texas; B.S., United States Military Academy, 1915; Army Tank School, 1921; graduate, War College, 1929; second lieutenant, United States Army, 1915; lieutenant colonel, Tank Corps, World War I; advanced through grades to General of the Army,

December 1944; Chief of Operations Division, Office of Chief of Staff, 1942; Allied Commander in Chief, North Africa, November 1942; Supreme Commander of Allied Land, Sea, and Air Forces in Western Europe, November 1943; Chief of Staff, United States Army, 1945-48; president, Columbia University, 1948-52; appointed Supreme Commander of the North Atlantic Treaty Organization, 1950; entered in presidential primaries on Republican ticket, January 1952; elected President of the United States, 1952; reelected, 1956; author, *Crusade in Europe*, 1948; *Eisenhower Speaks*, 1948. (See also *Current Biography: 1957*.)

GRUENING, ERNEST (1887-   ). Born, New York City; Hotchkiss School, 1903; A.B., Harvard University, 1907, M.D., 1912; LL.D., University of Alberta, 1950, University of Alaska, 1955; managing editor, *Nation*, 1920-23, editor, 1933-34; founder, Portland *Evening News*, 1927, editor, until 1932; director, Division of Territories and Island Possessions, Department of Interior, 1934-39; administrator, Puerto Rico Reconstruction Administration, 1935-37; Federal Emergency Relief administrator for Puerto Rico, 1935-36; governor of Alaska, 1939-53; elected senator from Alaska to work for statehood in Washington, 1956; United States Senate (Democrat, Alaska) 1959-   ; author, *Mexico and Its Heritage*, 1928; *The Public Pays*, 1931; *The State of Alaska*, 1954. (See also *Current Biography: 1946*.)

HERTER, CHRISTIAN ARCHIBALD (1895-   ). Born, Paris, France (parents United States citizens); École Alsatienne, Paris, 1901-04; Browning School, 1904-11; A.B., Harvard University, 1915; studied architecture at Columbia University; several honorary degrees; United States Foreign Service attaché assigned to United States Embassy in Berlin, 1916; special assistant, Department of State, 1917-18; secretary to American Commission to Negotiate Peace, 1918-19; executive secretary, European Relief Council, 1920-21; assistant to Secretary of Commerce, 1919-24; editing and publishing, 1924-36; Massachusetts House of Representatives, 1931-43; United States House of Representatives (Republican, Massachusetts), 1943-53; governor of Massachusetts, 1953-57; United States Under Secretary of State, 1957-59; Secretary of State, 1959- . (See also *Current Biography: 1959.*)

HORN, FRANCIS HENRY (1908-   ). Born, Toledo, Ohio; A.B., Dartmouth College; A.M., University of Virginia, 1934; Ph.D., Yale University, 1942; instructor of English and history, American University at Cairo, 1930-33; dean, Quinnipiac College, 1938-42, vice president, 1947; assistant dean, Biarritz American University in France, 1945-46; associate professor of education, Johns Hopkins University, 1947-51; president, Pratt Institute, 1953-57; president, University of Rhode Island, 1958- ; editor, *College and University Bulletin,* 1951-53; *Current Issues in Higher Education,* 1952; *Literary Masterpieces of the Western World,* 1953; *Twenty-Five Years in the Wide, Wide World,* 1955.

HUMPHREY, HUBERT HORATIO, JR. (1911-   ). Born, Wallace, South Dakota; student, Denver School of Pharmacy, 1932-33; A.B., University of Minnesota, 1939; A.M., Louisiana State University, 1940; graduate studies, University of Minnesota, 1940-41; LL.B., Law school, National University, Washington; assistant instructor, political science, Louisiana State University, 1939-40, University of Minnesota, 1940-41; member of administrative staff, Works Progress Administration; assistant state supervisor, later director of adult education in Minnesota; state director of war production training and reemployment, later chief of state war service program, 1941-43; assistant regional director, War Manpower Commission, 1943; professor of political science, Macalester College, 1943-44; mayor of Minneapolis, 1945-48; United States Senate (Democrat, Minnesota), 1949- ; visited the U.S.S.R. and interviewed Premier Khrushchev, 1958; member, Phi Beta Kappa, Delta Sigma Rho. (See also *Current Biography: 1949.*)

KENNEDY, JOHN FITZGERALD (1917-   ). Born, Brookline, Massachusetts; student, London School of Economics, 1935-

36; B.S., *cum laude,* Harvard University, 1940; LL.D., University of Notre Dame, 1950, Tufts College, 1954, Harvard University, 1956; served in United States Navy, 1941-45, awarded Purple Heart and other military decorations; correspondent, San Francisco United Nations Conference, British election, Potsdam Meeting, 1945; United States House of Representatives (Democrat, Massachusetts) 1947-53; Senate, 1953- ; author, *Why England Slept,* 1940; *Profiles in Courage,* 1956 (Pulitzer prize for biography). (See also *Current Biography: 1950*).

McCracken, Robert James (1904-). Born, Motherwell, Scotland; M.A., University of Glasgow, 1925; B.D., 1928; student, Cambridge 1937-38; D.D., McMaster University, Hamilton, Ontario, 1946; other honorary degrees from institutions here and abroad; pastor, Marshall Street Baptist Church, Edinburgh, 1928-32; Denistoun Baptist Church, Glasgow, 1932-37; associate professor and professor, Christian theology and philosophy of religion, McMaster University, Hamilton, Ontario, 1938-46; pastor, Riverside Church, New York City, 1946- ; lecturer on practical theology, Union Theological Seminary, New York City, 1949-54; associate professor, 1954- ; vice chairman, New York City Board of Correction, 1958- ; author, *Questions People Ask,* 1951; *The Making of the Sermon,* 1956. (See also *Current Biography: 1949.)*

Meany, George (1894-). Born, New York City; attended elementary and high schools, New York City; journeyman plumber, 1915; business representative, Plumbers' Local Union, 1922-34; president, New York State Federation of Labor, 1934-39; secretary-treasurer, American Federation of Labor, 1940-52; president, 1952-55; president, AFL-CIO, December 1955- . (See also *Current Biography: 1954.)*

Murray, Thomas Edward (1891-). Born, Albany, New York; B.S. in mechanical engineering, Sheffield Scientific School, Yale University, 1911; honorary degrees from many colleges and universities; Engineer of Year Medal, Yale Engineering Association, 1952; Laetare Medal from Notre Dame, 1952; Catholic

Peace Award, 1956; Cardinal Gibbons Medal, 1958; president, Metropolitan Engineering Company, 1932-40; president, Murray Manufacturing Corporation, 1946-47; granted some 200 patents in electrical and welding field; first impartial chairman, United Mine Workers Welfare and Retirement Fund; trustee, Bank of New York and Fifth Avenue Bank, 1933-50; director, Chrysler Corporation, 1935-50; Commissioner, Atomic Energy Commission, 1950-57; consultant, Joint Committee on Atomic Energy, 1957- ; author, *Nuclear Policy for War and Peace,* 1960. (See also *Current Biography: 1950.)*

NIXON, RICHARD MILHOUS (1913-). Born, Yorba Linda, California; A.B., Whittier College, 1934; LL.B., Duke University Law School, 1937; practiced law, Whittier, Califorina, 1937-43; attorney with Office of Emergency Management, Washington, D.C., 1942; lieutenant commander, United States Navy, 1942-46; United States House of Representatives (Republican, California), 1947-50; Senate, 1951-52; elected Vice President of the United States, 1952; reelected, 1956. (See also *Current Biography: 1958.)*

ROMNEY, GEORGE (1907-). Born, Chihuahua, Mexico (parents United States citizens); student, Latter-Day Saints University, 1922-26; University of Utah, 1929; George Washington University, Washington, D.C., 1929-30; associated with Aluminum Company of America, 1932-38; president, Washington Trade Association Executives, 1937-38; president, Detroit Trade Association, 1941; director, American Trade Association Executives, 1944-47; member of other trade associations and civic groups; Detroit manager and general manager, Automobile Manufacturers Association, 1939-48; vice president, executive vice president, Nash-Kelvinator Corporation, 1950-54, director, 1953- ; president, chairman, and general manager, American Motors Corporation, 1954- . (See also *Current Biography: 1958.)*

CUMULATIVE AUTHOR INDEX

An author index to the volumes of *Representative American Speeches* for the years 1937-1938 through 1959-1960. The date preceding the title of each speech indicates the volume in which it appears.